Essays and Aphorisms on the Higher Man

Emile Benoit

Eudaimon Press

Typeset in Garamond

Design by Jerry Urick

ISBN 978-0-578-07525-9

Eudaimon Press

2010

To my three best girls, with much love

L.M.B.

Table of Contents

Preface

This book is as much a work of art as it is philosophy. The essays and aphorisms contained within these pages are meant to inspire rather than impose, to incite rather than allow man to settle into a comfortable repose, delighted with himself. They are meant to inspire reflection and meditation rather than elicit some new form of control. While they are certainly intended to instigate thought and action, they are only suggestive of any particular course or direction that a man might choose. Therefore, they should be viewed as artistic or intellectual thought experiments, poems or ruminations of a sort that dabble in reason, but ultimately speak to something deeper in a man. After all, no rational theory can effectively answer the great mysteries of life definitively or provide direction for the variety of circumstances that arise in any particular person's life. I do not, of course, wish to deemphasize the legitimacy of reason's place in science, mathematics, or even morality, but theory, with respect to matters of spirit, soul, or character, is an unqualified captain for the task of steering someone to a deeper understanding of themselves. A person's self or spirit is something immaterial and subjective while the scope of reason oversees material and objective existence for the most part. Although reason may posit a number of perfectly logical and valid responses to a variety of the soul's concerns, it will ultimately fail to rouse the soul itself, which is more likely to be awoken by revelation and insight rather than rationale. The poetic nature of the aphorism allows for the most effective means by which to communicate directly with the soul of a man. It penetrates the protective shield of his rationality and reunites it to that part of his being which is most original and primordial — collective as well as individual, ancient as well as new.

The mystery that I'm concerned with in this book is the peculiar nature of the self, the human being, and the life best lived. Yet, the mystery of the self can be only unraveled by the person whose self it is; the life best lived can be only resolved by the person whose life it is. The following aphorisms are attempts, in their own small way, to motivate, as well as help guide, a man's unique and individual investigation into developing a kind of poetic or artistic perspective of the world, the awareness of the "higher man."

1

The State of Man

1

I am a madman in the same manner in which Socrates was mad. As Spinoza was mad. As Joyce, Dickenson, Blake, Weil, and Dostoyevsky were mad. All viewed humanity much as a child might view his father — glorious, courageous, full of integrity and promise. Yet, all eventually would grow disillusioned with the fact that man (or humanity if you will) fell far short of their expectation, a common lament that children everywhere often simply grow to accept about their fathers. Not these madmen. These idealists. They who would dare to snub their noses at wounded resignation. Their madness was a demand that their father fulfill his destiny. That he rise above the mediocre, the trite, and the banal in order to brave the heights of that which is excellent within him. In other words, these nobles would not let him sleep, delighted with himself and at ease with only the insignificant achievements that have previously sustained him. They were adamant, in some cases even downright incensed, that he claim his proper place in the universe, rather than simply inherit the laurels of his greatest ancestors and feed upon the somewhat naïve admiration of his children. These nobles would be of the sort that Socrates would term 'gadflies,' pestering humanity, rousing it from its slumber, a constant reminder that that which it has become is not enough.

2

I assume, and there exists very little in the known universe to make me think otherwise, that reality is made up of two distinct worlds. There is the world of thought or spirit and the world of sensation. The world of sensation is everything that can be measured by science. It consists of that which mankind sees, hears, touches, and smells. It is the world of "reality" as it is commonly understood by man. In contrast, the world of thought is the reality of the intangible; the reality of that which exists solely in the mind of man. "I," for instance, am a being who resides exclusively in thought. God is another.

3

Mankind's capacity to reason, when he chooses to employ it sufficiently, has provided him with a certain authority with respect to the world of sensation. He is able to control his physical environment to a large extent and rule what was hitherto unruly and foreign to him. Yet, the world of spirit, that realm of the irrational and disobedient imagination, remains a mystery because it does not adhere to the same laws of nature. In fact, it has little place for laws at all. Instead, it is governed by art which often proves to be a somewhat irrational sovereign.

4

Ideas are dangerous because they have a tendency to disrupt the status quo — to stir things up, sometimes for that sake alone. Needless to say, they are not the welcomed benefactor of the majority — those worshipers of mediocrity, fanatics of tranquility and the stable life. Ideas find their way into the social conscious only after they have been around long enough to become familiar. Otherwise, they are most often discarded with contempt or indifference. Of course, the difficulty always then, for the present, is sorting through the mire of the past to find those forsaken treasures. After all, not everything that has been rejected is worthy of recovery. Frankly, not everything that has been around for centuries is entirely worth keeping either, but that's another matter.

Ideas are also dangerous because they can throw one's psyche into chaos. No drug can lead to as much of a disastrous conclusion as an idea. Nothing has the capacity to decimate the protective walls of one's inner consciousness such as a thought. Thoughts are insidious. Their effects can be seen even among those who consciously battle against them — for anyone who shields themselves from a particularly frightful idea must, by necessity, gather a great amount of energy to finance such a war, often leaving the remainder of one's kingdom in ruin. And those that will, instead, allow an idea into their mind, letting it stretch out, recline, and become agreeable, risk the possibility of a psychological revolt — a complete upheaval of previously cherished values, opinions, and beliefs, leaving nothing behind to fill the void. As well, there is the danger that one allows just any thought to affect him so profoundly, to the extent that he is no longer discriminating. Instead, he overburdens his intellect and imagination with a collection of rubbish and pearls, of which he cannot discern one from the other. And all these dangers pale in comparison to the damage that can be done to humanity as a whole by a sick or unworthy mind that examines an idea and molds it to his own design, for the totality of the human soul is comprised of many disturbing and unruly factors.

Thus, I speak only to those wise, sturdy and determined spirits who aspire to reach beyond the commonplace and the everyday in order to discover something extraordinary about themselves; those cosmopolitan souls who are able to inhale the totality of existence and exhale all that would poison them. It is they, and only they, who might consider themselves worthy of admiration. The rest of humanity is nothing more than a glorified ant hill. Though these "men" may fancy themselves related to such luminary figures as Dickenson, Whitman, or Nietzsche, such an association is merely a figment of their own egocentric imagination.

5

Humanity, en masse, is anathema to the human.

6

Always beware of he who would agree with you

7

The modern man enjoys a removal from his darker nature. So much so that he can even blind himself into believing in the absolute goodness of his inner nature, banishing the more repugnant bastard child to the dank dungeon of the man's own subconscious to grow ever stronger. He is then shocked to discover the brutish nature of the child when it arises in the night from time to time. Yet, the brutality of the child is his own. A man should be first and foremost a strict parent to himself.

8

Animal and man have only one significant distinction between them: reflection—and this difference is only truly present in a modest minority of men, those who possess a certain "greatness of soul." Lacking this quality, mankind is merely an unpredictable, arrogant, narcissistic, gluttonous, rationalizing animal of the cruelest kind.

9

When deer overpopulate their habitat or some other animal lives beyond the limits with which nature has set, no man is surprised that starvation ensues among the deer or that a natural consequence occurs as a result of a transgression that exceeds the boundaries of natural law. Yet, mankind believes that these tenets do not apply to him and that somehow he will overcome the limitations of nature by the operation of his reasoning and the technological equivalent of a miracle. This brand of "enlightenment" thinking betrays a belief in reason that exceeds its own natural capacities and transforms science into something of a religion itself.

10

It is easier to love an animal than love a man. The animal has almost as many virtues and by far the fewer faults.

11

There is a certain terrible, sublime majesty to an animal as it cuts and tears apart his prey and roars at his achievement. In a man, the same action is repugnant because he must compare to the majesty of luminaries such as MLK, Shakespeare, Aristotle, and Voltaire.

12

The evils of the world originate within the heart of man. He only refers to demons because he doesn't understand himself.

13

Since there exists no purpose to a man's life or to the universe in general (at least beyond the mechanistic and biological drive to procreate and survive), a man must, if he wishes to do more than simply live the life of an insect, invent his own — though he should remain weary of falling prey to the lie.

14

Every individual man should identify himself with the whole of mankind since the whole is greater than its parts. From this perspective, the individual human destiny remains finite and limited, but the destiny of mankind can survive for unknown ages. The goal of the individual then is to participate in the Great Conversation of man and provide his own unique contribution to mankind as a whole. This is the closest he may ever come to immortality. However, to do so he will need to surrender his desire for individual aggrandizement and profit.

15

The idea that a man will benefit all of humanity if he firstly benefits himself is the egotistical delusion of the common man. It is an expression which is true, but only applies to a very few noble spirits.

16

The arc of mankind's destiny depends upon his aim.

17

Every species attempts to live according to their own conception of what conditions they find to be acceptable. Mankind is most comfortable when he possesses meaning. He will suffer the most unimaginable hardships if he finds these hardships meaningful and will not be able to bear even the most pleasurable and glorious of luxuries if he finds them hollow and pointless.

18

Man is limited on all sides except within.

19

A man will often claim the title of Man as if it were a special privilege of his birth. Yet, he must first be raised a man, study the greatest works of other men, and conduct himself like a man for the majority of his days before he deserves any special praise from the animals of the earth. In fact, more often than not, they look down their noses at him.

20

Man will very often renounce reason when he is most in need of it. He, too, will embrace reason when he has no need for it at all.

21

There is man and then there is the idea of man. The idea of man is the aspiration of man, the inspiration of man. Without the idea of man, he is nothing more, and often quite less, than an animal.

22

Based upon the superior accomplishments of others, a man awards himself the Nobel Prize. The nobility of humanity, however, must be proven with each successive generation and, even then, it is accomplished by but a very few.

23

God forbid that we should understand man as he is rather than as you would wish for him to be. As Hume declared about deriving "ought" from "is," it is similarly impossible to derive "could be otherwise" from "is."

24

Why is stupidity so often arrogant? It hasn't the good sense to recognize its own limitations which are all too often considerable. Or, perhaps it does recognize its limitations only too well and is thus blustering in childish rebellion against them.

25

Some 60 years later, the world is still recoiling in horror at the atrocities inflicted upon innocents by the Nazi party and individual citizens of the world. It seems that modern man simply finds it inconceivable that any human being or group of human beings would act in such a ghastly manner. This is only because mankind has largely forgotten the thousand fold other atrocities which would rival the actions of the Nazi's if not for a lack of technological capacity. I expect that the genocide in Germany will one day be forgotten too and there will come another terrible unleashing of that beastie "man" — no doubt surprising and horrifying his contemporaries as well.

26

A man should live as if his life were to be entirely scrutinized by posterity as well as the present generation of men – criticized and examined in exacting detail. It seems that he is mostly moral only when he knows or believes he's being watched – like a child he expects notice or punishment.

27

The writer who would wish to communicate with the "postmodern" man must of necessity write in aphorisms since the technologies and luxuries of postmodern life have incapacitated his attention span and he is no longer able to comprehend how these things might serve to hinder him.

28

Someday, in the not too distant future, your stupidity and your arrogance will wipe out the entire species of man prematurely. Shakespeare, Murdoch, Goethe, Shilling, Moliere, Cervantes, Newton, Aredant – gone. All gone. All memory of them will be erased from the tablet of existence as if they were nothing more than a smudge. If there were a newspaper left to record the event, the headline would read: "Mankind commits suicide!"

29

If a man truly wishes to abolish the stereotypes which sometimes serve to define him, he must first cease acting in such a manner. This will require at least a modest degree of honest reflection for a creature that is habitually unaccustomed to it.

30

The vast majority of men are little more than children without the excuse of youth to forgive them

31

"To live in the present moment" is nothing more than the sentimental idealism of the Romantics. It inspires men to indulge in all sorts of ridiculous distractions that do little more than reduce him to the status of the "silliest" of the animals. This idea makes of his life a trite and inconsequential event. It arises from an essential misunderstanding of the present as being an entity with little relation to the past or the future. Yet, the only present moment without a future is death and the only one without a past is birth.

32

Man has within him two natures — the animal and the divine. As an animal, man is among the most stupid and cruel in all of existence. As a divine, he is almost too scarce a specimen to acknowledge as existing at all.

33

Almost all men perceive themselves as somehow righteous and therein lies the blindness of their character. For the righteous are few in number and too virtuous to arrogantly consider themselves as anything other than souls in contemplation of the truth, rather than those in possession of it.

34

More often than not, a man will speak the most confidently about that of which he knows the least.

35

Man is engaged in a perpetual war with himself that, fearing self-destruction, he wages instead with the external world in the hopes of destroying those forces within that he finds so distasteful.

36

Man, as a social being, is the most distracted of animals.

37

Man is at his most content when his life resembles that of the domesticated dog – blissfully caught up in his own instinct, ignorance, and strict, unconscious obedience.

38

Humanity should not concern itself with making man less of an animal, but rather more of a man.

39

There has already been too much concern with man as the Ubermensch. I would be satisfied if man could simply become a mensch.

40

The only creature deserving the title "beast" is man.

41

A man cultivates what talents he naturally possesses and ignores or devalues those that he lacks. In this manner, the man who is endowed with physical attractiveness will do little in the development of his personality because he sees little need to do so.

42

The only place a man lives on after death is on the earth, either in his works or in the hearts and minds of those he left behind. At the moment of his death he becomes pure spirit, pure idea.

43

A man lives his life more out of subconscious habit than by conscious choice.

44

A man's fate is only revealed upon his death and most men hope that death will come quickly so that their destiny should not ever be revealed to them – so afraid are they of what it finally contains.

45

Man has become like a parasite, eating the flesh from the bones of his ancestors. His sense of entitlement is only exceeded by his hubris.

46

Only history will truly be able to tell the worth of a man — that is, if any remain who remember him.

47

Even the dying man projects his gaze to the future. His field of vision is only different in that it is measured in hours or days instead of months or years.

48

Man has the potential to play the role of the tragic hero but more often than not he plays the tragic fool. In literature, Willy Loman was such a fool while Oedipus was not. The difference between them? Oedipus was determined to act and know. He was unconcerned with consequences.

49

The spirit of the dead is nothing more or less than the collective memory of mankind.

50

A man with "thick skin" is usually a beast.

51

Man is not a rational animal but a conscious one. Rationality only comes later, if at all.

52

Those who believe that they possess an inherent dominion over the animals of the world severely overestimate their own capacities. They are the fool who thinks himself a king.

53

Man understands that the universe can be reduced to smaller and smaller particles, but he often fails to understand that the expanse of the universe into greater and greater elements is significant as well. Perhaps mankind finds it troubling to imagine his precious universe as nothing more than an atom on the backside of the divine. In fairness, amebas probably would have difficulty imagining themselves (if they could imagine) as nothing more than a minute element of man.

54

The idealization of the working man who is celebrated for his suffering, thankless labor is merely a form of consolation and control. All the world needs a ditch digger, of course, an unthinking, working drone, yet few want to admit that this is their fate and all that they might hope to obtain. Thus, a man's labors are given an illusory distinction that suggests that such a man is more than the tool of his society, often undertaken out of necessity by men whose minds are predisposed to such thinly-veiled forms of flattery.

55

There is much that man can learn from animals. Yet, he chooses only to imitate the fierceness and ignorance of the creature.

56

It is not reason that should hold the reins of passions, as Socrates suggests, but man who should hold the reins of both.

57

Life is neither entirely a war nor a struggle but that man himself makes it so through his own perspective.

58

The fearful are often more dangerous than the man who seeks to do you harm.

59

The only thing common about common sense is the commoner's belief in it.

60

The "cultured" man — that refined and literary man of taste and sophistication — is, more often than not, merely an external manifestation of a deeply hollow creature.

61

The man who loves himself in excess does not know himself at all. The same is true of the self-satisfied man.

62

A man more often uses his reason to rationalize his stupidities than he does to further his understanding.

63

The man who cannot tolerate the opinions and perspectives of others is expressing an inner lack of confidence in his own.

64

Psychoanalysis is yet another attempt in a long line of delusions meant to comfort man when he has been in some way confronted with the recognition of his fate.

65

Man carries on as if he possessed something of a free will because he has no other choice but to do so.

66

The life of man is a narrative for which he is the reader, but only tangentially the writer.

67

For every ill that man conquers, he generates another as a consequence. So, mankind never truly progresses against the ills of the world. He merely transforms them into another shape —perhaps one which he might better endure.

68

With a superior chuckle mankind scoffs at the industriousness and seriousness with which the ant struggles through his day, yet he expects that the universe look differently upon him.

69

Post coital remorse stems from the recognition that one's will is hardly free in any significant sense, but instead arises as a slave to certain passions and desires that lurk unexplored and misunderstood beneath the surface of consciousness – wild and uncontrolled, extremely dangerous if left uncultivated or ignored.

70

As a general rule, the greater mass of men are serious about those things which they should consider lightly and laugh at those things which should be treated with solemnity.

71

The entire existence of mankind is, has been, and will always be a kind of fiction.

72

I often wonder if mankind truly appreciates the majestic beauty of the world as he paves it over and rushes past it while weeping at the petty injustices done to him.

73

The one thing that the man of posterity is sure to remember is that he is more enlightened than his forefathers.

74

Only a fool believes that a man is intentionally self-created.

75

Man is only partially rational and even then it is usually in the service of one of his many prejudices.

76

Man's best side often appears simultaneously with his worst — wartime being a singular example. The hero who risks his life to safeguard a family of Jews appears alongside the mindless Nazi drone who seeks to assert his superiority through their destruction. Yet, why should mankind let his best lie dormant when the world is momentarily at peace? The best of man rises from adversity.

77

Man destroys nature in the name of progress and in so doing brings about his own decay.

78

Mankind has reached such a state of hubris now that it threatens his very existence on the planet.

79

A man can never be and should never be devoid of ego. However, he does need to fashion a means to master his ego and understand the limitations of the thing. He must honestly assess his merit as free from egotistical prejudice as is possible and not let himself be duped by the praise or estimation of others. Otherwise hubris is the result and one transforms from a strong and powerful individual to a blustering fool. He who thinks highest of himself is often already lost.

80

Man is mostly unconscious in the day to day activity of his life.

81

Mankind secretly hates science because it suggests too much of the truth to him, namely, that he is of little more consequence than the rabbit or the turtle — how much more significant man wants to be than the nameless, faceless snake in the grass. Yet, he must accept these conclusions if he wants to demonstrate any true value to his existence. Then will he possess the kind of greatness that shows itself within the majesty and magnificence of the wolf, tiger, bear, or lion — a greatness of character that is connected to who these creatures are within — they cannot be otherwise. All animals possess their own unique greatness of character except for man. He must first wrestle with his consciousness of death, put aside his fears, and reject the magical lies that are generated to make him feel distinctive and somehow immune to ultimate defeat. Only then can he be considered heroic and worthy of mention, fleeting though his time may be.

82

If you speak only to a man's spirit and offend his mind, he will be upset with you. If you speak only to a man's mind and offend his spirit, that, too, will draw his rage.

83

Awake! Awake!

The enemy now does ride!

Upon your backs do the scoundrels fly!

84

Mankind is nature's memory. She experiences everything through him.

85

Before a thing can fail, it must succeed to try. Failing *that* is the ghost that haunts most men as they sleep.

86

The memory of man is sporadically defective. It's as if it were somehow tampered with, having every third word removed as a matter of protocol — thus preventing a man from returning to his past with any reliable accuracy.

87

Up from the slumbering bed of dreams awoke the human being.

88

The chains of nature are a blessing; the chains of man, a sin.

89

Society's ode to the common man celebrates that which makes him common but ignores what truly makes him great — his stoicism — and only this latter quality should give cause to celebrate the man.

90

There is really no need to find fault with the color of a man's skin, the quality and quantity of his possessions, the way he speaks, or the manner in which dresses, when his character is so readily at hand.

91

All men shall one day die, their ashes scattered to the wind and their remains buried in memory. That is, if memory remains on earth — that will require that man remain first.

92

In their struggle for material equality, women have unwittingly lowered themselves to the level of man.

93

While man may speak and reason, and thus determine himself superior to the animal, he more often than not uses his speech merely as a means to express his *lack* of reasoning. It serves as more of a growl or a grunt than an expression of any special significance.

94

Mankind secretly abhors nature because it preys upon the weakest member of his faculties; the ego.

95

Man assumes that the flow of evolution is upward in a straight line and it is he who resides at the peak. Yet, it is just as likely that the movement of evolution is circular and man rests upon the downward arc.

96

Rationality is, more often than one might expect, the irrational act of reason.

97

The man not able to find his greatness in poverty will equally fail to come upon it in wealth.

98

When an animal is defeated by a superior, he will submit. When a man is defeated by a superior, he will submit in show, but spend the rest of his days, if necessary, in an attempt to find victory by some other means, even if the method be delusion. This can be either the greatness of man or a product of his childishness, depending on the circumstances under which he fashions his rebellion.

99

<u>Mused the feminine to her sisters:</u>

We sisters are but passionate fools!

Led by the heart on to any dark horse

that champs at our bit. Let him be sleek

and shiny, or muscled, quick and svelte.

Let him be bred by a stallion, or smart

and artful in his stride, or gallant bearing

leaders of nations, maidens in distress.

Let him be a mustang, savage and free

Or better still, soft and endearing,

or crippled, enticing our sympathies.

But all in all he is an animal!

Why should we sisters become weak in the knees

at the sight of every passing dobbin?

Rather we should make them all a gelding.

It would make for a more smooth and pleasurable

ride, no doubt, a more gentle companion.

Yet our hearts betray such violent means.

The eyes of a colt at the sight of our blade

would cause us to blush in tearful empathy

and we would fall to love again. Damn

that trickster nature. Damn that beaming maid.

If only love were made less of putty,

of a sterner metal, marble, or brick,

and not this lump of velvet clay that tempers

to the touch of any supple finger.

It would endure; fixed in effigy

for the admiration of the multitudes.

Yet, for the soul, cased in iron, a tomb.

No man shall send me thus to somber grave,

ungrateful beggars, sucking at my tit.

For I am lithe and bonny. Yes, relenting

in my passion but headstrong in my care.

I whisper, yes, to sweetness, but to fear

and malice I am like the screaming wind.

So treat me not as if a bauble,

though I may seem fragile, a porcelain dish,

I am a woman, soft, pliable,

able to rend the heavens with my kiss.

And you men, fearful dissenters ever,

haven't the courage to be blessed with my

most precious gifts.

100

Man's trouble is that the totally impertinent becomes terribly important.

101

One of the most dangerous enemies of a man is his own ego, although the egos of his contemporaries rank rather highly as well.

102

The majority of misery, anxiety, anger, resentment, jealousy, and hate that exists in the world arises from a man's refusal to accept the circumstances of fate which are beyond his control. Modern man is the anti-Job.

103

To read the works of the great artists and philosophers is to participate in a kind of festival of man, such that it provides the reader with a feeling of deeper belonging to his species which is often otherwise missing from his daily interactions with the beast.

104

The hubris of any present age is the belief that they are the most enlightened of all who came before them. From such blindness arises the notion that all of culture has been aligning its stars for their arrival.

105

A man's life is predicated on chance and lucky circumstance more than he would ever care to admit, so he gives himself credit for his luck. Yet, the fact of the matter is that were it not for one blind shot by his father, overcome one day in a moment of unexpected and uncharacteristic passion, that happened to hit the mark, the child would never have been born to crow about his glorious achievements.

106

It turns out that reason and logic are simply, or perhaps I should say, "complexly," just another game designed by man to play with his universe.

107

Human beings are not motivated by self-interest but by their perception of self-interest which requires a significant amount of interpretation and analysis of any particular circumstance to render an aim or decide upon a direction. Given that men are for the most part deficient in their employment of reason, overabundant in their subjectivity, and overweening in their egotistical estimation of themselves, it is no wonder that they are predominately unpredictable, unstable, dangerous, and incorrigibly stupid.

108

A man's worst feature is his ego which rewards him more than his due and deludes him into believing that he is so deserving.

109

The world is a quiet and peaceful place only when the majority of men are sleeping in their beds.

110

Modern man has created for himself a world in which his spirit cannot live unless anesthetized by drugs, distractions, or religion. In this manner the human being in him, the man, is left to sleep while the beast goes about his day, whistling a tune and avoiding all things that might reveal to him a reflection of himself.

111

I have stared into the waters of men's souls and found them to be depressingly shallow.

112

The manner in which a man struggles with the limitations of necessity will often reveal a great deal about the character of the man since it is through these struggles that one develops character. The struggles in which he *chooses* to engage himself reveal even more about the man and will ultimately determine the course of his destiny.

113

Man is born free but often chooses a kind of slavery as a means to an easier life, one absolved from having to choose altogether. This is not accomplished, however, through some singular, dramatic decision between freedom and slavery. Rather, one makes a myriad of seemingly insignificant decisions that all effectively eliminate choice in one way or another. No one particular decision determines whether a man will find himself alienated from his own heart in this manner — since it is the collection of these similar types of decisions which ultimately lead to a man's relinquishment of his freedom — but every man's destiny is aligned with a certain variation on a theme.

114

The beastliness of the hunter, that which makes him something *less than* an animal, is not to be found in the hunt, the kill, or the eating of meat. His beastliness rather stems from his enjoyment of the kill, his relishing of it, and the childish celebration of what he perceives to be his omnipotence over life itself — all this while steely-eyed as to the true consequences of his action.

2

The State of Nature

1

Who shall rejoice in the memory of man once his kind has been extinguished from the planet? No one. Nothing. It is therefore the responsibility of all generations to act in such a manner that allows for successive generations to exist — else all are destined to be prematurely forgotten for all eternity.

2

A man esteems himself so highly and blows up his worth beyond all proportion because he secretly knows that nature will one day wipe his existence from all record.

3

Men need to extricate themselves from the notion that they are the protectors of their families or nations and begin to realize, with Heidegger, that they have a much finer universal role than this, that is, as protectors of nature. The earth could just as randomly be a cruel and unforgiving rock in the solar system, uninhabited by anything resembling life at all. Yet, man seems to take his life for granted, as if he were endowed by some inalienable right to his existence. This is where his arrogance, his hubris, and his inability or unwillingness to change his perspective will bring about his downfall.

4

If a man does not bow in awe to nature, to the sublime beauty and seeming orderliness of the mystery itself, and worship it with all the fervor of an evangelical priest, then no God ever conceived will do much to truly impress him – for he is no doubt dead to the world.

5

The man who hates nature cannot help but despise himself as well, closing himself off from the source of his existence and embracing, instead, a universe that is entirely foreign to his essence — the city.

6

If the cosmos are perceived as a living being, and I would suggest that it should be perceived as such, then what is man to it usually but a parasite? Does he not wish to be something more? Or is his imbalance the disease with which nature must contend forevermore?

7

The only values inherent to nature itself are moderation and balance. Thus, a man should learn to highly prize these qualities in himself and cultivate them into his life since he, too, is a part of nature.

8

Man has spent the majority of his time attempting to control, tame, utilize, and restrain nature so that it might be harnessed for his purposes. In so doing, he has desecrated the land, polluted the skies, poisoned the waters, and eviscerated the animals — all for the sake of his own selfishness. It is his own *inner* nature which is most in need of taming and from which he draws little in the way of resources that will sustain him beyond a few more generations.

9

Nature is cruel, unforgiving, and intensely indifferent to the concerns of mankind. The man who perceives nature as something beneficent or personal is merely deluding himself for the purposes of surviving in a world which has no need of him. Likewise, the view of nature as *only* cruel, unforgiving, and indifferent negates its capacity to inspire.

10

It is much easier, less noble, but ultimately more efficient to destroy than to create. What nature took eons to bring to fruition, man destroyed in a single millennium.

11

The sufferers of the Holocaust (as well as those similarly situated), they who were forced to confront the reality of mankind's terrible savagery (fueled in part by his indifference, arrogance, and stupidity) were, no doubt, struck one day by the contrasting beauty of a sunset or a sunrise and the realization that there is something quite unnatural about the will of man.

12

Man thinks more highly of himself than nature ever will and for that affront he makes of her a bitter enemy. Yet, as the old folk tale advises, one should consider one's enemy as something of a true friend because only he will tell you the truth.

13

The only illusion inherent in the appearances of nature is man's belief that nature is something of a superficial facade and that a truer, better world exists beyond the realm of the senses.

14

Divinity is possessed by all things meaningful and mysterious, all things that resonate with some deeper, yet mystifying, significance – love, for instance, or inspiration. The Greeks were attuned to this idea and theirs was a world more alive with meaning because of it. They had a plethora of Gods because each mysterious and meaningful thing possessed a divinity all its own, unique and individual. These were not the once removed creations of a single divine Being, merely fractions of a greater whole, but divine unto themselves. Every animal had a certain divine nature, every tree, every forest, every man – a multitude of Gods within a complex and mysteriously divine universe.

3

The State of Truth

1

The man who says he has found the truth has found nothing of much significance. Perhaps he's discovered a portion of the truth. Perhaps he's only stumbled into a wealth of fact. However, the truth can never be contained in a single volume, or be related in an evening's conversation, or even offered finally in the ruins of a brilliant man's work. To believe that science has even scratched the surface of truth is to live in delusion. To think that it ever will is an optimism born of a minister's wife. Those who would prescribe to narrowly follow the tenets of any one particular branch of knowledge or religion deserve the least credibility. For they seem to have exhausted their search before it even began in earnest.

2

There is no inherent meaning to nature. At its core, life is chaotic and wholly unpredictable. The teleological belief that there is purpose or a final design to nature or mankind has been imposed upon the universe by the imagination of man since he finds these conditions to be somehow necessary for his own existence. Yet, meaning is nothing more than an invention of man. It is his natural habitat wherein he thrives — as the eagle is most glorious in his habitat of the sky, so too is man in his search for meaning.

3

Answers, in one's search for meaning, serve as a means to multiply the questions. An answer, in and of itself, is always incomplete. Therefore are those who are satisfied with an answer to the extent that they cease further inquiry also incomplete. This is the essential problem of being. When one is no longer in the process of becoming; that is, questioning, re-evaluating, searching, and dissecting even their most cherished values, ideas, and beliefs, they are, essentially, no longer living. One only *becomes* anything in death. To *be* is to be always in the process of becoming something else.

4

No system of thought (including religion and art) will ever contain the entirety of truth, a landscape so rich and expansive that it is impossible to narrow it into a mold fitting for publication or public viewing. If one intends to embark upon a quest for truth and/or meaning they should not expect to find it blithely sleeping in a manger, or carved upon some stone on a mountaintop, but, instead, scattered to the wind in an infinite number of different pieces.

5

Songs Your Mother Sang

What system of thought causes a mother to sing to her child? If she were to think on it might she not fall into despair? After all, the child begins to age as soon as it is born. She, too, is dying. And if she lives long enough to see him grown, invariably he must leave her. And this she knows, though she may deny it. Whyfor then the song? And why a tune so optimistic? A sound so full of hope? Her hymn is one of justice, though none she will receive. Of unity, though the two shall be forever split. Of eternal love, though by consequence she must relinquish it. Wherefrom springs her courage in the face of such a bitter foe? She fights against the forces of gravity and so, by leaping from these heights, her descent will show to be all the more crushing. Whyfor attempt it? These are deeds which confound our reason. Yet we understand them. For the soul doth know things for which even gods throw up their hands.

6

Truth (and, likewise, meaning) resides in the imagination of man – reason, of course, being but one category within the imagination. Universals are such only in that they are common characteristics found within mankind's imagination. As such, they are universal to man alone. A man is what he imagines himself to be as he strives to achieve (or should so strive) the apex of his imagination. To stretch one's imagination is to stretch oneself.

7

Truth is never an answer to anything. It is rather always a hypothesis.

8

Cannot everything be traced back to an abstraction? Isn't that reality? At the every least, abstraction or thought are different modes of reality than the empirical validations of the senses.

9

Shakespeare wrote that "there is more to heaven and earth than can be dreamt of in your philosophy" — and thereby one reason to disdain any categorical estimation of truth.

10

It has been said that ignorance is a condition, but stupidity is a choice. This is often an important distinction between the adult and the child as well. The former has simply chosen to accept his ignorance; in fact, he often views this kind of stupidity as something of a virtue. Yet, the higher man knows that he is provided with no excuse for his lack of understanding and attempts, instead, to lead himself to greater awareness.

11

If the whole of nature were devoid of any meaning whatsoever, man would still seek it passionately because meaning is a necessity for him. Even when one is resigned to a meaningless universe, this resignation fulfills a kind of understanding.

12

Only the very best things have little or no "practical" application.

13

Mankind lacks more than it will ever possess.

14

The moment that something becomes "known" with certainty, a man should take great pains to retrace his steps to discover where the trail has led him astray.

15

Ministries of delusion — purveyors of falsehood, censorship, ignorance, and stupidity — are perhaps the most prevalent in the present age than they have ever been in the history of man. Of course, mankind has long lived in a state of ignorance and stupidity, censoring himself with falsehoods. Yet, only recently has he cultivated a perspective of the universe wherein he is able to clearly see certain errors in his previous thinking. Herein swoop the ministries of delusion to entertain and further stupefy the masses so that they might not feel the pangs of a spiritual evolution.

16

The "truer" reality, the "other" world as it were, is precisely the realm of the imagination wherefrom springs reason, substance, mind, and sense experience.

17

I say there does exist a different reality in the form of the abstract. The abstract is the realm of Plato's "Forms," though hardly an empirical kingdom in the sky. We know the abstract in this worldly reality of ours but the abstract essentially resides in the reality of the mind, a different plane altogether — the kingdom of thought.

18

Kierkegaard claims that there can be no system possible for human existence. The beauty of literature is that a completely enclosed, meaningful and destined existence *appears* to have been created in the work itself. It is the illusion of a complete and purposeful world that mirrors the inner world of man and makes him believe that his external world, too, is likewise magical.

19

Organized religion arose when man lived essentially by his passions alone. The ordainment of reason slowly began to elevate science as a new kind of religion. The evolution of the species will be when man can incorporate and digest all of his religions and live wholly, honestly, and peacefully with himself and others. It will be a time when he accepts all of the religions, arts, and sciences as expressions of human greatness; a time when even truth will no longer be an eternal proposition but simply an expression of mankind's prominence at making the incomprehensible understood — if but only briefly.

20

Man finds it difficult to comprehend a chaotic and irrational universe because it disposes of so many of his cherished and hard won beliefs. He has a prejudice, a strong prejudice, that keeps him from accepting anything but a view of the universe as somehow comprehensible or at least promising comprehension. Any other perspective makes him anxious and moody.

21

The universe can be perceived in a dewdrop

22

In the sense that man makes meaning from nothingness, he is similar to the God who creates the world from nothing.

23

The principle of multiplicity is that there are a complex multiplicity of Gods, truths, and perspectives that unify man's understanding of the universe. There are a multiplicity of fates as well. A man would do well to embrace those perspectives, truths, and Gods which best lead to his own individual flourishing.

24

The multiplicity of truth, while indeed a conclusion that there exists not merely *one* universal truth, does *not* support the conclusion of relativity — the idea that all perspectives should be valued equally — since this will depend upon the type of man attracted to any particular perspective. However, a man should become keenly aware that the knowledge that he possesses about *anything* of real value might just as well be false as it is true, especially his most cherished principles. Therefore, it should engender a kind of intellectual humility in a man and a moderation in his behavior.

25

The superiority of Socrates, the wisest man of Athens, arises from his silence as much as his questioning.

26

The only truth that most men desire is the one that they can live with.

27

The Great Conversation is the dialectic that seeks to determine praiseworthy perspectives from those which go against the grain of human sentiment. The former perspective man deems as good and moral, the latter is reasoned to be bad or evil. No one perspective is inherently good or bad, they merely are distinguished by mankind as one or the other based upon his assessment of the situation at the time. The questions that remain, of course, arise in trying to determine the good from the bad given the many aberrations found in human sentiment. If three quarters of humanity believes that killing is wrong and the other quarter is either indifferent or actually enjoys killing, how does a man reach a consensus on the matter? By a simple majority? Leaving aside the impossibility of counting the votes in such a case, it seems difficult to accept the notion of majority rules with respect to issues of human sentiment since it can be so widely varied. The Great Conversation is employed here, not as a once and for all signifier of truth, but as a method for arriving at understanding and wisdom with respect to the significant issues facing humanity. Toward this end, the great works of the past are consulted and the present perspectives of learned men are weighed along with the more thoughtful responses of the common man (if some exist).

28

He who knows will find it difficult to tell and he who doesn't know will speak so passionately and profusely that one would swear the man must know something. Alas, such is the dilemma posed by speaking with one's neighbors.

29

A man of certainty knows little more than that he feels certain and almost nothing of what he imagines himself to be certain about.

30

Art, philosophy, religion, and science are all designed to give meaning, reason, and stability to the universe in order to understand that which is inherently a mystery.

31

A boisterous opinion is usually a symptom of ignorance.

32

It's no coincidence that those things which man *determines* to be useless *are* useless.

33

While it may be true that the mind is nothing more than a whir of electrons sparking in material space, that which it ignites is some-thing altogether immaterial.

34

Man mistakenly views the transitory nature of his existence as evidence that there is something inferior about it. Yet, the only thing that possesses any permanence whatsoever is temporality and as such it is something inherently valuable – without it, value itself would either cease to exist or become nothing more than a trinket. Imagine how bored a man would be if everything remained static. Imagine the man who remains unchanged since his boyhood days — the pathetic soul who never experienced the quiet beauty and wisdom of old age.

35

To lament change is to lament life itself.

36

The problem with being in love with truth and the right is that a man can often become blind to the flaws of his beloved and begin to defend even the most unscrupulous of whores.

37

Pragmatism is the philosophy of surrender.

38

Nothing is meaningless unless a man deems it so.

39

Nothing endures, so man should learn to love the changing.

40

Wisdom and understanding will always be the commodity of the few. The majority delight too much in their stupidity and superstition for it to be ever otherwise.

41

Free will is merely a pretense. Man resembles the whirling stars more than he does a creature that is self-directed — except, of course, when he creates.

42

The evil inherent in any particular doctrine is the underlying expectation that one should follow it. It is better to mine bits and pieces from all doctrines to form one of your own. This is, after all, the manner in which all established doctrines were formed in the first place.

43

The world behaves, in many cases, to mankind's perception of it.

44

Man should not follow the example of Descartes and doubt everything except clear and distinct ideas, but everything *including* clear and distinct ideas. For notions such as these are nothing more than ideas that he *believes* to be clear and distinct.

45

The world makes more sense to man poetically and musically than it does intellectually and thus he believes the former must be true. This is due in large part to his failure in developing his intellectual capacities.

46

In the waking world there exists little proof of dreams. In the dreaming world there is little proof of the waking. Consciousness alone unites these worlds together.

47

A learned man can be just as ignorant as any ditch digger. Know this before you applaud yourself for your wisdom.

48

Nature plays with science as a cat does a mouse, allowing it a chance to breath, to regain hope, before snuffing its life from him.

49

Meaning is in the eye of the beholder — even a meaning in meaninglessness.

50

Anyone who has experimented with hallucinogens will describe to you the change in perception that occurred for them with respect to the spatial, temporal world around them. The world that they experience in this state appears vastly different, sometimes even surreal and only unreal if compared to their knowledge of the world that they left behind before they ingested the drug. Yet, both worlds exist in the reality of perception. It is only the perceiver, the interpreter, that has changed. Each of the separate worlds exist simultaneously with the other. The hallucinogenic perception will, of course, be devalued as an incorrect conception of reality since it was conceived through the lens of a substance that alters "normal" perception. However, "normal" perception is no less screened by particular elements of the human brain. If man had the brain of a dog, he would view the world as much more of an olfactory experience. If he had the brain of a fly, he would view it as refracted in hexagonal patterns. Kant, of course, remarked that mankind can never be sure of the "thing in itself." The experimenting with hallucinogens at least can allow one a different perspective than the one to which he is born. However, this applies, as does everything of significance, only to the man of character. A lesser man will merely find terror or titillation in their use, leaving him either forever scarred by the experience or lost in the siren song of oblivion.

51

Anything known for certain to be true can only be the truth of the moment.

52

How might you remember yesterday if you don't believe in ghosts? What of tomorrow?

53

Simply because a man creates meaning doesn't necessarily mean that it is something worthwhile or beneficial, something that would provide significance to the entirety of his life and inform every aspect of his existence. One can find some kind of meaning through the playing of sport, for instance, and perform excellently in that regard yet not be participating in what is most worthwhile. The lesser man will often find his life in such meaningful trivialities. The higher man seeks to find in life something of a more primary meaning to his short existence, the kind that leaves all the rest seeming trite and superficial. The kind of meaning that used to be found in the worship of God, but now must be realized elsewhere.

54

Perfection exists solely in the mind of man, not because he has any direct experience of it, but because he desperately desires for the world to be so.

55

Science explores and illuminates the practical and useful aspects of reality and calls its findings "truth." Yet, it is a truth of a rather superficial variety, allowing for only partial insights into the complexity of the human character and providing little guidance as to how a man should live out his life.

56

All of philosophy has arisen as the result of a series of evolving thought experiments.

57

The great myth of science is that it shall one day provide the solution to all of mankind's most enduring troubles — all disease shall be eradicated, all misunderstanding made clear, and all delusion brought to light. It is for this kind of technological utopia that man now yearns.

58

Pragmatism, that defeatist philosophy of utility, itself becomes a kind of truth and leads one to the perspective that everything can be perceived as existing merely as a tool — as a means rather than an end, as Kant would say.

59

Man is often led astray in his assessments of himself and his world because he fails to perceive the multiple dimensionality of existence. Rather he sees things one dimensionally — black or white, hot or cold, dead or alive. He does not possess a poet's eyes because he chooses not to view the world in such a manner.

60

The universe is not ruled by reason, though man would wish it were. There is orderliness to be sure and certain patterns do exist, but fundamentally it is a system of chaos altogether unfathomable to the human mind. So when a man examines the world for rhyme or reason, he is essentially creating poetry.

61

The awareness of complexity is often a far more valuable aid to understanding than the simple answer to a question in that the latter may not inspire further questioning. The man of wisdom may possess fewer answers than the man of common, or even supreme, intelligence, but he does possess a much keener awareness of complexity.

62

The absurdities that are sometimes reached with philosophical theory demonstrate the difficulty of incorporating reason itself in determining truth. This is not to say that *reason* is absurd, only that the utilization of reason alone is insufficient.

63

A portion of man's fate, sometimes an essential portion, is decided by sheer random accident. He may search for the reasons why he was either cursed or blessed by chance after the fact, but the answers can never satisfy him for they are not rooted in the rational.

64

Most philosophers are unaware that they are participating in an art form. Scientists, too, are merely artists working in the medium of proofs and experiments. Truth and meaning are, after all, creative constructions of human consciousness.

65

To understand truth one must first recognize the distinction between it and "facts of the matter" at issue. Facts of the matter are simply empirically or otherwise scientifically verifiable phenomena. The earth, for instance, moves in an ellipse around the sun. This is a fact of the matter which leaves itself open, admirably, to alteration should some new understanding arise. The arrangement and compilation of such facts should be referred to as knowledge. Truth, on the other hand, is something more directly connected to the human being himself. It is a brute fact of the matter that a man exists during a particular point in time; that he possesses certain genetic features; that he has a body which works, for the most part, in harmony with itself, etc. However, the truth of his existence is something much more personal to him, something that cannot be empirically verified or scientifically quantified, but must be reasoned as well as intuited.

66

The rabble who debase reason as a power which deserves little reckoning almost always do so, if they have not altogether lost their faculties, by fashioning reasons for it. A man without his reason is little more than a fragile butterfly enjoying the summer's day without realizing that soon the winds shall blow and he will be forced to flutter far from his intended course.

67

Curiosity did not kill the cat, it was conformity.

68

It has long been assumed that reason and emotion are separate entities. Plato suggested that reason should be the driver of the two wild horses, appetite and passion. Yet, the passions inform a man's reason as surely as reason has influence over the passions (love being the most obvious example). This is because the process of reasoning involves emotion in some significant way.

69

At the quantum level, everything is relational, which simply means that there are no individual things in the universe; there is merely one. This is typically a Buddhist perspective with which quantum physics has begun to agree. It is the consciousness of man which allows him to reflect on himself and make it seem as if he is a creature somehow separate from the whole, but he serves as the sense of awareness and contemplation for the creature with a billion eyes (nature) — unless, of course, he chooses to be a kind of parasite instead.

70

A man cannot help but to find the world meaningless if he fails to passionately engage himself in it. He would similarly find himself imprisoned in a loveless and superficial marriage if he failed to willingly and whole-heartedly commit himself to the idea of sacrificing to such a union. After all, nothing of importance ever came to fruition without some kind of forfeiture to man's adoration for his beloved. Yet, if a man is unable to find anything in the world in which to passionately devote himself, he is either too lazy to search for it or mistaken about the wellspring of his own heart.

45

71

If Schopenhauer truly believed the pessimistic conclusions of his philosophy, then his ideas seem strange when communicated in writing since writing itself betrays a belief in something meaningful. Yet, it's interesting to note how viscerally men react to pessimism of any kind, as if such observations can be dismissed on the grounds that they do not correspond with man's conception of his own nature.

72

Oftentimes a man will apologize for a comment that he claims he didn't mean to utter. In a state of passionate emotion, for example, he makes a choice to lash out at a friend by telling this person something that the man had been keeping secret in his heart so as not to offend. He claims that he simply wasn't thinking clearly at the time when the words slipped from his tongue. Yet, what he's really apologizing for is speaking the truth. In such a case, reason is used as a tool for deception, both to deceive himself and others. Emotions, as Sartre argues, are simply different means of perceiving the world. They are also inherently more honest than reason.

73

Life is only absurd according to a man's reason.

74

In Plato's Phaedo, Socrates discusses the example of a fish that believes the ocean above to be all there is to his world until he peeks his head above the surface to discover the realm of air, sky and dry land. Furthermore, the fish can see that this newly discovered world is so much better than his own in that it brings him "truer" perception. Similarly, Socrates thinks that men perceive their world as established and well understood, but if they were to reach the limits of the atmosphere, they too would discover a "truer" world than their own. Yet, Plato does not seem to consider that this type of heavenly abode is itself limited and able to be transcended. His perception of it as a "truer" world than his own is merely the human tendency to equate a newer understanding with truth.

Perception, however, has no limit since it originates within the human imagination.

4

The State of Happiness and Fame

1

Imagine a drug which would allow the person who ingests it to feel profound pleasure and even perceive himself to be supremely powerful while providing the illusion that he is wildly admired and a character of significant achievement. All this he would experience without a hint of doubt that this was his reality and it would last for the entirety of his natural life.

Of course, most men would prefer to encounter these things in the world of time and "reality" since they feel this would be a truer and more valuable experience than occurrences that take place merely in the mind. Yet, how many of these men will ever actually experience anything even close to the effects of the drug in their daily life? This is the question that will begin to gnaw at them over time. As their own personal reality begins to differ more significantly from the reality that they know the drug to provide, they will begin to weaken their stance about this truer world. Gradually, they will begin to view reality itself as a kind of illusion and choose to take the drug themselves and there they will live forever satisfied.

The higher man, on the other hand, understands life differently. He will not choose to ingest the drug because he does not value its effects. The illusory nature of the world is of little concern to him as he knows that all perspectives are tainted with illusion to one degree or another. The reality of the mind, he further reminds himself, has a certain truth all its own which a dreaming man would not deny. Yet, the benefits of the drug he does not perceive to be of any benefit at all as they would make of him a slave to his desires. While they were being fulfilled, he would be ruled by them entirely, overtaken in a kind of heavenly oblivion. If he managed to somehow break free of their control, he would forever be haunted by the memory of such desires fulfilled and all his life would become pale and lifeless by comparison. Either way, he remains a slave.

2

A man's life never loses its meaning; he simply expects that it should mean more.

3

Distraction and delusion are a kind of suicide.

4

Love is a path that should be chosen only by the heartiest of individuals to test their stamina and philosophy with life. Happiness is brief in love and replete with suffering. Anyone who chooses love as a means to happiness is likely to be extremely disappointed with the result since happiness itself is significantly short-lived and fickle. Instead, a man should seek out a lover who serves as a kind of foil with whom he might assess his mettle – a modern conception of the old medieval notion of trial by ordeal.

5

There is a beast that cries "I want" over and over while clawing his way up the side of a sheer rock cliff. The words "satisfaction," "happiness," and "comfort" are etched upon the pale beads of pearl strung around his neck like a choker.

6

You fat, well-fed, happy fools will come by your death as something of a surprise while your life, in retrospect, will be completely lacking in value of any kind. You are the "stuff with which to fill graves" who, being still embalmed, will fail to nourish even the worms. Despite this all, you will no doubt chortle on your deathbed like a boorish school boy.

7

The Greeks and Romans seemed to enjoy discussing happiness as if it were some kind of eternal or consistent state of being which the "good" man acquired. Happiness, however, is fleeting for everyone. The good man naturally has days, months, or even years which are perhaps only minimally happy and the evil man can experience precisely the opposite. Happiness is not a goal; it is a temporary state — sometimes acquired simply by accident of fate or as a momentary basking in the present condition of one's being. A man might look back on his life and determine it to be happy overall, but he will be conveniently forgetting or dismissing a large portion of his life that was bereft of happiness altogether. The only man who is consistently happy is the simpleton who is either completely ignorant of his own state of being or possesses little in the way of desires for his life, wishing nothing greater for himself than easily attainable little pleasures. He is content because he is amused.

8

Do not be so naïve to think that the stupid, the ignorant, the corrupt, and the wicked are not happy — sometimes deliriously so.

9

Long term happiness, an overall feeling of prolonged satisfaction, is a sure indication that a man's aspirations were set too low.

10

Stupidity is often masquerading as happiness.

11

It would seem, given that there is no overall purpose to life except that which man has created, that hedonism would be a reasonable solution as to how a man should spend his time. After all, if nothing possesses any ultimate value, then the happiness that is generated by pleasure appears as an acceptable consolation. However, pleasure, as the purpose of man, is inadequate —not because pleasures are fleeting but because they are trifling. Pleasure builds to nothing and leaves its practitioner no better off than he was previously except for a momentary feeling of satisfaction which demands of him to revive the sensation again and again. Often one is left feeling a slave to pleasure.

12

Happiness is a fleeting condition, a momentary joy that is soon replaced by some other state which floats in the ether of human emotion. Its acquisition, furthermore, is quite often not in one's control. Thus, to possess it as an aim is akin to an attempt at mounting a shooting star.

13

The optimist views the world as he wishes for it to be while the pessimist views the world as he suspects it might be already.

14

A kind of convenient forgetting is essential for happiness.

15

Suffering is the debt that one pays for consciousness.

16

Men consistently and intentionally delude themselves and call this happiness.

17

Items of luxury and fashion are the pacifiers and rattles of the man-child.

18

A man surrounds himself with companions often as an unconscious and vain attempt to arm himself against the assassin of time — as if, by sheer number, the fiend will be warded off.

19

The recognition that all life is suffering is not a surrender as some profess, nor a mournful cry of the disenchanted. It does not absolve man of his responsibility to be just and to attempt to instill justice in the world. It is simply an acknowledgement or acceptance of the fact that despite a man's efforts, suffering will persist. This should only serve to make a man less likely to despair that his efforts are all for naught. He is, after all, battling with the very nature of the universe. He must know from the outset that he will ultimately lose his battle if he might be considered heroic.

20

Man is content in all the wrong ways, with all the wrong things, and for all the wrong reasons.

21

In order for mankind to live a life of depravity and wastefulness, superficiality and ignorance, and arrogance and artlessness, he must first believe that when all is complete, he will have acted in the service of some greater good. It is precisely the utopian ideal of happiness that leads a man to such conditions since more often than not he will believe that happiness *is* such a commodity.

22

Melancholy is not a disease and has no need of a cure. It is a fitting reaction to the temporal nature of the world for man. Giddiness and happiness are the true afflictions, similar in character to blindness.

23

There is no joy in paradise, only boredom.

24

If a man is able to fulfill all of his dreams by the time of his death, he has no cause to celebrate. Such an accomplishment merely demonstrates the paucity of his imagination.

25

A man will not choose to subject himself to slavery, not because it might restrict his freedom, but because it might limit his happiness, as he conceives of it anyway. Yet, he will gladly make himself a slave *to* happiness.

26

The great man, the virtuous man, is no happier than the lesser because he keenly senses the tragedy of life, the bittersweet melancholy of existence. This makes his life more profound to be sure and he feels the overall profundity of life to a significant degree. It fills his entire soul with a sense of import and weightiness, one which arises from his perspective. The man who chases after wealth and all the other external niceties suffers from a lack of proper perspective and while he may be happy for a considerable period of time, his life feels ultimately devoid of overall significance – so much so that he must build alters to his success or to his

God in an attempt to convince himself that he is something more than a simple lump of tissue.

27

All men are indifferent to those things which they believe to be of little value. Yet, most men value exactly those things towards which they should in fact remain indifferent.

28

Bred into the American society of equality is the mythic notion that any man might raise himself to the heights of superiority and excellence. However, when he too quickly discerns that he possesses no such qualities within himself, he fumbles to still achieve the myth in some fashion. Thus, he seeks to acquire those things which make him *feel* seemingly superior — fame and riches. Since the majority of others also sense their own inadequacies, they too aspire for that pinnacle of mediocrity — material success. It is a culture that celebrates its own least excellent feature and takes vengeance upon what is truly excellent about humanity.

29

Fame is often mistaken for the ultimate validation for a life well lived. A kind of reward for the man who has made the necessary sacrifices and now enjoys the spoils of his well deserved destiny. Most men view fame as a brand of success that will somehow live beyond him as well as validate his entire existence. On the contrary, it is often only a reminder to him that his life was actually not much more than a shallow facade.

30

In matters of greatest importance, it is generally not the cream that rises to the top, but the foam.

31

Fame is the bastard child of Character. It is his father's *reputation* that Fame desires, not the reasons for it.

32

Fame is actually the achievement of fate, so no man truly deserves any credit for it.

33

Only the shallowest souls find fame to be anything more than a tremendous burden.

34

The man who seeks out fame is similar to the child who seeks parental approval — both are lacking in the ability to validate themselves.

35

Your moon is the same as Newton's moon, the same moon that enabled the tide to wash Shakespeare onto the shores of the earth and drag Mozart out to sea. Yet, too, it pulls you and countless thousands into the deep abyss anonymous.

36

To possess a great soul is reward enough for the man who has developed it. Though he may be touched by fame, he knows never to seek it out since the ambition to be recognized distracts the great man from the focus of that which makes him great.

37

As a man gets older he will begin to notice that little which was championed or celebrated in his youth has survived. The greatest actor has been forgotten and the shocking and controversial piece of art has become little more than a silly museum piece. Such is the fate of all men.

38

You, the living, shall soon join the ranks of ghosts, spirits, and others who have long since been forgotten and exist now as haunting figures that terrify the living man who strives to be immortal.

39

Pay no mind to those who are praised or even deified by your contemporaries — full many a "genius" has been undone by the accolades of his admirers. After all, significance is only rarely glimpsed in the moment. Spectacle, on the other hand, as well as "originality" are more often perceived in the now and misunderstood as greatness.

40

Most men seek fame as an antidote to the mediocrity of their lives. Alas, it merely serves to further the disease.

41

Have you ever heard tell of the great warrior ant that went by the name of Mettelus? Or the magnificent philosopher dung beetle, Gippenshire? Then why do you suppose the cosmos might be interested in you?

42

As a man pays homage to the heroic actions of the bed bug, so, too, does a meteor honor the accomplishments of man.

43

Fame is a multi-headed beast who chooses its victims almost entirely by chance.

44

The man who pridefully hoists his trophies or celebrates his accomplishments has never contemplated the size of the galaxy in which he sits nor the minuteness of the galaxy within the universe entire. How one finds it easy to laugh and make sport of this doodlebug for the seriousness of his labors and how difficult to note the similarities to oneself.

45

The mass of men will never recognize those who exist on a plane far above them in character. They will only elevate those that they admire and since they do not admire or value the truly greatest traits of man, they will not promote or celebrate them to any significant degree — at least not with respect to their contemporaries. The mob will acknowledge the man whose name and works have been passed along for centuries, usually by the labor of a very few, because they possess a certain reverence for the dead and are usually too timid to contradict history.

46

Success and fame are no more a validation of merit than giving birth is an indication of good parenting.

47

Fame makes a man a slave to his celebrity.

48

More often than not, the man who strives for worldly success has found little of it in his own heart. This is also true of the man who aspires to success in the afterlife.

49

Every old man knows, has lived to witness, that all fame is fleeting. The young all clamor around it because they mistakenly believe that immense fame is something immortal and unchanging. "These are the truly great!" they think naively, "Their kind will remain with mankind forevermore." These children have yet to experience the sight of a passing comet — known briefly by name and then forgotten. They are as yet unaware that most of the legendary, renowned, and celebrated men of their time will have their stars dim and vanish within their own lifetime. The rest will disappear shortly thereafter.

50

Do nothing in attempting to elicit the admiration and praise of your contemporaries since praise and adulation are heaped mostly upon those who are undeserving.

51

Disgrace is a state of mind rather than an external determination, although the latter often informs the former.

52

All fame is man's attempt at consolation and all consolation must necessarily ignore the fact that even the name of Aristotle will one day be nothing more than the dark matter of the universe.

53

Those who value leaving behind their name or deeds for posterity to ponder hope to be remembered as an empty shell. If one's name or deeds were the important elements of a man's life, he could conceivably begin at childhood to pitch a stone with his name written on it into a pile and achieve immortality by constructing a huge quarry to himself by the end of his days. Yet, I'm afraid that soon enough posterity will wonder how to rid itself of the eyesore.

54

The reason that so many men would sell their souls for fame is because they believe that they have successfully bartered for a bargain. Yet, the man who values his soul as anything other than priceless is probably either correct in his assessment or misguided by his perspective.

55

Be wary of fame for the mob does only rarely give praise for worthy things and then usually only when the recipient has passed away.

56

He who possesses a worthless soul will gladly sell it for a chance at fame. Yet, he will quickly find that he has purchased only a hollow statue and has overpaid for it too.

57

The worship of celebrity is the negation of oneself.

58

If man knew the amount of randomness that was involved in conspiring to lift him to fame, he would forever cease mentioning his talents.

59

Beware of they who would make of you a hero, rather they will make of you a slave.

60

Worldly greatness is not a trifle because it is fleeting or otherwise subject to the randomness of fate, but because it adds nothing to benefit the essence of a man and often severely distracts him from his more fruitful projects.

61

The self-respecting man is often merely a man with low standards.

62

The modern man has great difficulty recognizing the genius' of his time, so expecting is he that they should arrive with spectacle and fanfare rather than ridicule and derision.

63

A grown man worships heroes because it allows him to abdicate his responsibility of becoming one himself.

64

The vast majority of men, in any age, are little more than fools. To wish for fame, then, is merely the desire to be admired by fools, making a man a fool himself. A man should hope, instead, to make something of himself that he imagines would be admired by the great men of antiquity. This requires him to relinquish the notion of *being* famous altogether and focuses him instead on the task of evolving.

65

It's difficult for a man to conceive of himself as the hero of his own life when his part is, or appears, rather insignificant on the stage. The starring roles are those which he firmly believes to exemplify a life well lived, heroic and inspirational. Yet, his character is what defines his status as a man. There can be as many feeble Hamlets are there are glorious Guildensterns.

66

There is such a thing as immortality but it differs greatly from the sort that most men might desire; that is, the eternal manifestation of his consciousness, his legacy, or his memory. Immortality, instead, has to do with the eternal nature of Being itself, of which any individual man is but a small, unconscious part. The spirit that arises into consciousness from the void returns its energy again to the eternal radiance of oblivion — a small consolation to those who might simply wish to live forever.

67

It is a waste of time for a man to pursue his happiness if he is utterly unaware of what constitutes it within him. He should be pursuing a better understanding of himself foremost.

68

If a man must become famous, it is better to do so posthumously so that he is not around to witness how posterity will treat his life and his work. There are immature souls, of course, who desire to forgo any sort of work that does not lead to fame, fame itself being the goal of any endeavor they decide to undertake. These small, un-ripened minds hope to find some external and rather superficial validation to a character that is lacking from within. Yet, their fame will do little to fill the void in their heart and, instead, create an ever widening chasm between the world within and the world without. So much so that he will find that his character has been developed *for* him and resembles his inner self only tangentially. Of course, small minds are so enamored with, and immersed in, distraction that they may hardly notice the fundamental essence that is so lacking in them.

68

Journalism is rather similar to the jottings of a man who follows around a fourteen year old boy, diligently recording everything the lad utters.

69

The rabble rank mediocrity and excellence by the estimates of achievement and material success because these are quantities that can be easily measured by others. Yet, mediocrity of character and excellence of spirit and intellect can only be truly measured by oneself since they are essentially private understandings. This proves too unsatisfactory for the man of the mob, accustomed as he is for approval from the hoards, and too complicated as well since he prefers the concreteness of simple numeric quantifiers to the abstract computation of logarithms.

70

Removing consciousness and reflection from experience would no doubt lead to a happier life in that a man could be engaged, but ignorant. Yet, he is entirely unable to remove himself from the conscious reflection that this type of existence would not be a good life for him. Consciousness and reflection are, instead of qualities that hinder a man, necessary in order to be considered one. More often than not, however, men desire to be asleep or unaware, working so diligently to achieve happiness instead.

5

The State of Death

1

It is believed that a man cannot simply live as if he were to expect his death tomorrow. He has too much responsibility toward his future self to be so rash. This assumes, of course, that the life one currently leads is unsatisfactory and that the knowledge of one's demise would bring with it cataclysmic changes to the ends that one pursues. However, this is the beauty of death. It can show a man the way to his true character. It can lead him out of the paper castles that he has made for himself and onto the path of redemption. If he were to feel the need to quit his job, then it is a profession that he was not meant to pursue. If he were to feel the need to travel, then he has waited too long to explore the world and he should now venture forth. If he were to feel a sudden desire to spend lavishly on himself or others, then he has merely played the role of miser though he was not miserly in his heart. If he should feel the urge to kill, then that, too, has been an element of his character and the belief in his own morality proves simply an illusion. The man who expects his death at any time will leave this earth with little left unfinished, while the man who saves his talents for a rainy day will find that he has so safely filled his coffers with nothing but regret.

2

In the great hurly-burly of life, death intrudes to show that the entire cosmos is truly silent at its core.

3

Heaven, as it is understood from the scriptures, is nothing more than oblivion itself, a place that one resides in complete and utter unification with the divine — a state wherein one loses their recognition of ever having been an individual.

4

It is frequently proclaimed and celebrated of the newly deceased that they put up a "good fight" against death at the end. Yet, in the fullness of life, such vigor and resilience is often found to be sadly lacking.

5

Mankind seems to adore the underdog as a kind of revenge on death since death holds dominion over all. The idea is, of course, that one can somehow win out over the most prominent opponent of them all. Yet, sadly, this is merely childish fantasy. Courage in the face of certain death no more signals the immortality of the human spirit than cowardice might. The very concept of immortality is the balm of Gilead that the sick utilize to bring themselves to health again, not realizing or caring that it is a placebo. "It works!" they cry and concern themselves with little more. They would cover themselves in excrement if they believed that it would heal. Courage for its own sake they do not recognize as a virtue because they possess so little in the way of virtues in the first place.

6

He who would find death to be a release is either suffering some kind of torture or has suffered a kind of death of spirit that simply awaits the physical manifestation of the inward state. The latter is the spiritual state of the religious man.

7

To denigrate the body because it changes and does not endure is to denigrate all of existence — including the soul — since everything that exists has been and will be something different than it is at any present moment. Change is to be exulted and celebrated by he who values life. To value the changeless and immutable is to value death and nonexistence since these are the only things that remain untouched by alteration.

8

These houses that you've built, oh man, spot the horizon like graves stacked one upon the other for as far as the eye can see because you have no regard for moderation — neither in your personal life nor your social organization. You cry from the mountaintops, "more life!" yet you produce from the factories more death.

9

The living are always right, but the dead have all the answers.

10

Death is life's only gratification and contentment. In fact, those who wish to spend the majority of their days seeking to be gratified and content are suicides of sorts in that what they ultimately seek *is* death.

11

Modern man is in love with death, though he is unaware of his desire since he truly fears the beloved. After all, he will readily admit that he loves his drugs, his orgasms, his tobacco, his shopping sprees, and his entertainment. These, however, are the ornaments of the beloved. Man is so afraid of what he truly desires that he is not able to gaze his loved one in the face, but must settle for merely these reflections.

12

Time heals all wounds since he eventually kills all of his patients.

13

It would seem as if most men live too long. The sheer duration of their years lulls them into a kind of apathy that fetters the wings of action. By the time a man comes to truly believe in his own mortality and see what an utter waste he has made of his life with respect to matters of deep significance, he is quite too old to do anything about it.

14

Death adds a certain significance to a man's life — sometimes more so ever than it had when he lived.

15

The lie about suicide is that if a man proceeds where he is not invited, upon arriving he will find a gruff and impatient host. The only host, however, who resides beyond the walls of time is oblivion.

63

16

What is another joy more or less when dust be the final destination? The answer will differ depending upon the character of the man.

17

A man is afraid to die only to the extent that he is afraid to live.

18

Each morning a man is awoken from the dead and offered an opportunity for a new life.

19

Life is too short at the ends and too long in the middle for the majority of men.

20

There is a rather morbid sense of superiority and arrogance that the living seem to feel toward the dead, almost as if those now deceased had been outlived.

21

All men will surely die, that is certain. Yet, the man who occupies his life with trivialities will hardly recognize a change.

22

The eradication of man will seem redundant once he allows himself to be completely removed from nature and his own humanity.

23

Nature, which first gave birth to man, is slowly devising a way to be rid of him since he has proven himself a menace — an arrogant, stupid, useless, selfish, near-sighted menace.

24

If someone were to ask you to provide for them an answer as to what might make their life worthwhile, you will find that after extolling certain virtues and recalling specific joys, you will soon exhaust yourself. There is no precise solution. The mind hasn't the capacity to arrange the infinite into a few simple defining features. Man has reason. Life does not. Nor has it any meaning other than that which is imposed upon it.

25

It takes no great courage to face death. Any drunken fool can do it and everyone will do so eventually. To face life, however, to strive to achieve something which you are aware has only itself for an advantage and even then only briefly, takes courage.

26

A clock strikes midnight, spreads its wings and flies away

While sleeping children whisper the gospel in their dreams.

A demon lurks in the shadows kissing newborn babies goodbye.

Souls, disemboweled, wander aimlessly

As the sun is swallowed by the cold, cold moon.

Where do the deer run to in a forest fire, a blazing inferno?

Are the rabbit's holes deep enough that they might hide?

Smoke is rising on the horizon, coming near, coming near.

The devil lights his cigarette and laughs while

God throws up his hands and Jesus cries,

And the Buddha claims he doesn't give a damn.

The end will not come by expectation, my children, but slowly, gently, rocking you to bed.

Keep your eyes on the watch and feel yourself falling deeper and deeper,

Relax, still deeper, feel yourself letting go.

You're getting sleepier and sleepier, no longer fighting.

Tell me the truth — are you really all that afraid?

Why have your friends all abandoned you today?

They look at you now stranger than you've ever seen them.

Is that father McGinty, praying for your soul?

Doesn't he know that you're not going anywhere?

Mother — where are you?

Father — why do you run? I'm your only son.

Honey — don't leave me here all alone.

It feels as if you're floating in a dream

And all the things that you have seen are but figments

Of your imagination.

27

Your age is of the season winter, my friends, when the withering daydrum of the uncouth masses is heard in verse through the sickly wails of a beaten dog. The December freeze of your polluted seas taints the once crystal glacier a muddy brown and these decades seem bereft of great spirits to bestow warmth upon your condition. So that you now of numbing hope, frostbit unto the heart, shall flock to any spark of smoke that might burst from it a fire. To ashes you pray, from dusk to dusk and day to day. The frozen soot of once so brilliant flames now fanned by fools who seek to blow alive again that passion, yet for their own greedy aims.

28

Children are often perceived as being especially brave in the face of death. This is hardly surprising, prone as they are to believing in fairies, angels, and magical beasts. Theirs is an overly optimistic and simple perspective of the universe. It shelters them from life's more abstract and severe qualities with which they are as yet unable to cope. Children, of course, can be forgiven for this weakness in their character. A man, on the other hand, has been too long separated from the womb to believe himself courageous in taking such a stance.

29

There are a great many means to suicide, only a few of them resulting in actual death.

30

When a man's reflections on death are relegated to the dark corners of his subconscious mind, his life appears less sacred and divine and its direction becomes less significant as well.

31

Death will often strike in the most banal of times and demonstrate that even banality may hold a deep significance for a man.

32

A terminal prognosis will often shock a man into perceiving the world from the artist's perspective. It arrives, of course, better late than never. However, how much of life was lost in the interim?

33

The dying man has no time to bother with the petty, superficial, and meaningless distractions that occupy the lives of the common man. Yet, you are all dying men, so amend your life!

34

It's not as if men are no longer afraid, as they were when they were young, of the monsters in their closets. They merely call them by another name — the enemy, the other, death, and change.

35

The man who does not want to die before his time means to say that he wishes to be afforded at least as much time on earth as the rest of his contemporaries. He will take no comfort if he lives beyond the years that were provided, on average, to the man of ancient times since he understands the fruits of human progress to be his fundamental right. It is only the comparison to his peers that interests him and fuels his childish sense of justice, refusing to accept a lesser share of anything.

36

Death is the humbler of all men's glory.

37

A man is never victorious over death since everything perishes with him. At best he can win a few small battles along the way. Yet, victory only rarely reveals the character of a man while losing almost always reflects something of his true nature.

38

Any day now will strike the reckoning time, so if you have something to do with your life, you'd best do it quick lest the long, boney fingers of doom arrive to whisk you away to nothingness forevermore. Awake! Awake! Fate is rapping at the door and asking that you account for your existence. What shall be your answer?

39

Old age is essentially a rather unnatural occurrence that has only in modern times, because of man's own interference, come to be regarded as something "natural." The majority of men, after all, never reached old age during ancient times. Likewise, the death of a child is only "unnatural" given the modern man's perspective that his technology has somehow caused nature to bow before him.

40

Man only deems death a necessary end in order to make it seem more reasonable. If there's anything a man cannot abide it's the irrational nature of the world. Yet, the man who finds it reasonable that a child should die and in such a manner that he suffers greatly in the process, as has happened more times upon the earth than could ever be necessary, is seeking solace from a world which provides none itself. In so doing, he is blinding himself from the truth and establishing expectations which are themselves unreasonable.

41

The man who is unafraid to be alone, in fact rather *choosing* that company over any other, will find death to be nothing altogether terrifying.

42

Men often claim that they would be miserable if they somehow came to be immortal since it would provide them with no escape from the world and eventually lead to a wretched and unhappy boredom. This is most probably true for he who has no real love of life.

43

The only providence to death or life is that which a man will make of it, thus creating the illusion that it were so.

44

Is consciousness alone, brief though it may be, not enough of a gift to accept the terrors of extinction and the brevity of existence? If you were woken from the abyss, years before your birth, and offered a short respite from the unconscious restraints of nothingness, would you not be grateful for the opportunity?

45

It's one thing to have nature decide the time of one's death. It's quite another to have it decided by man since he possesses no rightful authority other than that which he has fabricated through disingenuous reasoning. Immediate self-preservation is the only truly justified foundation for killing that nature would sanctify and, even then, not the kind that is coldly calculated and rationalized by portly men in their armchairs. Thus, the condemned man ends his life in a state of greater righteousness than his executioner.

46

The man who commits suicide, in one form or another, when he might otherwise be engaged in something beneficial to himself or others, deprives the world of something which it most desperately needs — his participation.

47

The suicide (whether literal or metaphorical) lacks a passionate commitment to any one particular thing in life. It's no small wonder that a failed romance so often precipitates the final act of a desperate man.

Lacking as he is in passion for anything other than this one little bird name Eros, he can quickly become despondent when he scares the bird away. Unless, of course, he finds some other means more fundamental to his constitution toward which to focus his attention.

48

Those who would decree that the man who is terminally ill should not be allowed to take his life have no regard for life itself but merely its appearance.

49

The death of a friend or associate, especially if he dies young, will give a man pause and cause him to reflect upon the brevity of life. At first, he will swear to spend more of his time at leisure, treating his life as something of a game to be enjoyed and savored. Yet, this too shall pass and he will soon find that he has fallen into another kind of rut, the hollow routine of retirement. The gift bestowed upon him by the death of his friend, that which shocked him to awareness, was something sorely missing from his existence and quickly became forgotten once he fashioned upon a solution to it. It would seem that awareness and reflection are anathema to a man.

50

A great many people are introduced to the proper way of living through a protracted process of dying. In coming to realize the actuality of their own death, they will begin to naturally become reflective about the state of their existence. So, through this confrontation with death, a man will come to see what should have been his life.

51

A man should view all tragedy that befalls him as a kind of gift that affords an opportunity for a new, truer perspective of the world — sometimes for this purpose alone might tragedy reveal itself. Yet, a man must first alter his perception of tragedy. If he views it always as a thing to be avoided, then his perspectives will remain relatively unchanged from childhood and his vision of the world, and all of its inhabitants, will be largely one dimensional.

6

The State of Religion and Maturity

1

What if this was the only world you were to ever know? What if it were true that when you die you are simply banished from existence for eternity? Let us imagine that there is no God. Whose life then would still hold meaning for him? Would it not be those exemplar spirits, those eternal rebels who would press onward regardless — morally, excellently, not out of some delusional denial but, instead, from a profound, heroic sense of self? Is that not what we mean by "God"? Faced with the abyss, surrounded by isolation and meaninglessness, He created meaning.

2

They, who would recoil in horror that without God "everything is permitted," are more fearful of their own natures than those of their neighbors. Religion has provided them with an inner restraint that is lacking moderation of its own accord. They are desperately in need of laws and regulations to their behavior since they are essentially children. They may have departed the home of their parents, but they have only exchanged it for the dwelling of the state, the embrace of popular sentiment, and/or the bosom of the church. They more desire to live in comfort and mediocrity than to expend the necessary effort toward individuation. If "everything *were* permitted" they would be, essentially, homeless.

3

One should give no more attention to the opinions of the devoutly religious than they should give attention to the beliefs of the young — both are lacking the kind of wisdom that should come with experience. The young simply have not yet lived long enough to gain such wisdom. The religious would rather live their lives in comfort and contentment than suffer the necessary pangs of truth. Both must be humored, distracted, and intellectually ignored.

4

It is best that one first understand that their time shall soon enough come to an end and it will end for all eternity. Man should not allow himself to fill his thoughts with comforting nonsense such as heaven, immortality, or some Nirvanic bliss that shall arrive after death. Death is certain. It is final. It is likewise all consuming. To understand this complexity and to accept it courageously is the starting point which then may propel a man to actions worthwhile and meaningful. To concern oneself with what shall happen to one's soul after death is to clutter the mind with pointless speculation which will quickly serve as an obstacle to the true mission of one's life — the cultivation of one's soul while alive.

5

What is hope but a desire for some final destination? Final knowledge. Final confirmation. Final end. Hope, in essence, is a desire for death.

6

The world might actually become a tolerable place if Christians spent more time fashioning their lives to the true example of Christ, that is, toward the idea, rather than believing in him.

7

In the new "modernity," religion takes place only where idiots consort with fools.

8

Philosophy differs from literature only in the sense that literature is readable and understands that it is literature. Philosophy and religion are literature with delusions of grandeur.

9

The fact that Christ chose unlearned men for disciples suggests that the Christian has always been a kind of sheepish herd animal, more concerned with obedience than wisdom.

10

The devoutly religious man (the fool) attempts to disguise his clownishness by donning the garments of the saint atop his jester's bells. Yet, if you listen perceptively enough, they can still be heard to jingle.

11

Nietzsche had it wrong in one respect at least. God isn't dead. He's irrelevant.

12

Instead of man aspiring to reach the Gods, Christianity lowers God to man.

13

Man has no concept of eternity. It is, like a dream, ultimately incomprehensible. If pressed to examine the eternal, man's mind wanders to the limits of his understanding but surrenders the task once he grows weary of the boredom inherent in the concept. He then draws a line there and calls everything beyond that point the eternal. However, the eternal is nothing more than a dream — a vain hope to somehow understand his death (another dream) in context. Eternity itself can be found in the moment as well as its duration.

14

Eternal death should be the concentration of a spiritual man since the hope of eternal life degrades the spirit. Eternal death illuminates the notion that man is at the mercy of the unknowable and inconceivable, thus unspeakable, nothingness. It inspires a person of consequence to creatively forge meaning from chaos. All too often, however, men who are of lesser spirits (presumably because they've failed to put their spirits to the test on other occasions as well) will cower before such a thought and surrender to ideas which are more pleasing and delightful.

15

All of Christianity is merely a poetic restating of Plato's thought.

16

Humanity abhors complexity and adores leisure and peace of mind, so it should be no wonder as to why mankind favors religion.

17

The Christian fool has for a brother the nihilistic fool. For the nihilist rejects his own intuition in order to ordain the world as essentially senseless and devoid of any meaning whatsoever. Yet, he himself has found meaning in his own claim that life is devoid of it.

18

The Jews seem to understand the paradox of hope much better than do the Christians. Judaism is a religion based on a hope for the coming of a messiah that they secretly do not wish to see arrive for it would bring an end to hope and destroy the religion itself. This is why they deny Christ as any kind of savior. It would signal the end of all that they hold most dear. The Christian, on the other hand, impatiently awaits for just such a day.

19

There is today a mass movement that has the religion of popular sentiment or culture at its core. It, too, is populated with fanatics, ecstatics, and priests who all revel in the spectacle of self transcendence — a whole cacophony of suicides.

20

How often have I heard a man proudly claim that he is able to determine right from wrong, as if morality were simply a mathematical formula to be committed to memory. In this the insane man, who purportedly cannot make such a distinction, appears saner than the moral judge.

21

Responsibility is absent in a dream. All contracts are null and void. There is no accountability, no recourse, and no rule of law of any sort that can reasonably be determined. In short, it is heaven.

22

The Jews didn't crucify Christ; it was the supporters of the status quo —
those sad spirits who are so fearfully abhorrent of change. It was they
who are Christians today. They are the anti-Brutus. They would rather kill
to prevent the disarray of established dogma.

23

If the truly great man is he who is least understood, then what does that
make of the devil, who must surely be the most misunderstood of all?

24

Indeed there were witches and devils among the townsfolk of Salem,
though they were often mistaken for elders of the church.

25

"Forgive them, Lord. They know not what they do" sayeth Christ up on
the cross. Why should they not have known? They certainly could not
have known that Christ was the son of God — only a child or a fool
could believe *that* with any certainty. However, they surely should have
known that their actions were barbarous. No matter if all three of the
supposed criminals were in fact guilty of their crimes, nailing or tying
them to a cross to have them die in the desert sun is nothing short of
arrogant barbarism. Arrogant in their self-satisfied belief that they are
somehow morally superior to the criminal and barbarous in the delight
they take in meting out the punishment. Man often excuses himself for his
ignorance, yet his ignorance is often a choice he has made for himself.

26

A majority of the established religions of the world make it impossible for
a man to be moral since one only acts rightly in order to achieve some
eternal reward or avoid some eternal punishment. The will to act in a
moral manner is corrupted from the beginning.

27

To anticipate the end of the world with anything but a sense of dread and
trepidation is to betray a hatred for those souls who were truly the greatest
representatives of humanity. The common man harbors a perverse,

though unconscious, desire to erase mankind's existence from memory — to reduce Shakespeare, Emerson, Homer and Ovid to the same elements of dust of which he is made. Extinction is his revenge on the elites for having the audacity to rise above him.

28

And an angel of the Lord descended upon the pious and said, "Behold! You must change your life!" And the pious all bowed and mistook the angel to mean that they should pray more dutifully.

29

You will find that there exists no purpose to the universe except for your own purpose for it to possess one.

30

Why does the Christian set eternal punishment among the flames? It is because he feels more at home in a cold, passionless surrounding.

31

One can really only banish oneself from "God." Ironically it is the devoutly religious man who has managed to do so with such consistency.

32

A man must remain unprejudiced about prejudice as well.

33

Moral certainty is the certain sign of a fool.

34

"God" should only be understood in metaphoric terms – that is, as an idea or an interpretation rather than as some kind of feeble persona. Only then can religion have any significant value for mature individuals, as a culture of Metaphorists.

35

The absence of a meaningful project in a man's life has a far more debilitating effect than the absence of "God."

36

"God" and the "Devil" are no less real or fictitious than one's own "self." All are abstractions that have been created by the human mind to explain and organize human understanding and serve to help a man transcend the banality of his existence.

37

When the great mass of men find it difficult to live up to the high standards of their religious tenets, they do not seek to better themselves but to interpret the religious texts in such a way as to lower the standard and artificially inflate their own standing.

38

Those who profess to sanctify the virtues of "family values" do not possess a value that is deficient in others — man is, after all, a creature of tribes. What these purveyors of fanaticism truly value is rigidity and the desire that everything should remain as it is for all time.

39

Any attempt to *believe* in art as the religious have made it their habit to do and defend its productions as being demonstratively true, historic, or unequivocal laws is merely the product of a simplistic mind that is ill equipped to comprehend the more subtle, and certainly the deeper, aspects of art itself. These childish minds read Shakespeare as if it were a fable of Aesop, that is, superficially and without notice of the varying (and infinite?) complexities that dwell beneath the surface of the work and make it worthy of consideration in the first place. Institutional religion deals in superficial interpretations and thereby has an appeal to only those souls with little depth themselves. I hesitate to call them children since it gives children a bad name. After all, the child has an excuse for his lack of depth and understanding — conceivably they will one day grow into a more mature individual.

40

The western man has set for his life a childish purpose while the eastern man has designated himself as having no purpose at all.

41

If, as Emerson states, it is true that to be great is to be misunderstood, then the devil would seem to be the greatest of all since few are so misunderstood as he.

42

The testing of Job was not the devil's intent. Instead, it was to deflate the ego of God.

43

Sentimentality is often mistaken for compassion. Christianity, for one, bases an entire religion on this mistake.

44

The Christian is under the mistaken belief that he needs to somehow deny or punish his own animal nature, but this does not separate himself from the animal at all. It merely makes him one of the more pathetic of beasts.

45

Some of the greatest thinkers and artists of the world have been the devil's advocates since they are purveyors in the art of possibility.

46

The difference between the devoutly religious man and the contemplative man is that the religious man seeks only that others should contemplate and should do so in the manner to which he prefers.

47

The religious man hopes and prays because he lacks the courage of Oedipus to seek out the truth.

48

Fundamentalism, in all its many aspects, should be rooted out of man like a choking weed. Yet, the individual man himself is the only one who can accomplish such a task. The application of force in order to achieve these ends will only deepen a man's resolve to entrench himself further in his own severe rigidity of thought. So, he must be inspired to undertake such difficult work and leave behind the comforts of certainty.

49

To worship is to over inflate the value of something in relation to oneself.

50

There are three types of men, essentially — the comedian, the tragedian and the sage. The comedian is the fool who believes that all will be resolved to his satisfaction in the end while the tragedian is all too consciously aware that the only resolution to life is death and oblivion. The sage, on the other hand, knows that comedy and tragedy befall upon the fate of every man, each in their own time.

51

Religion is an institution of the afflicted.

52

The child who believes himself to be the offspring of papa God vastly overestimates his significance in the infinite universe.

53

God "died" long ago for most, but people still gather 'round the corpse that illumines like a dead star. They stare at It because It gives them contentment while they await for It to speak.

54

For those that are not called to greatness of the soul, let them take comfort in their religions and innumerable other distractions.

55

A society alleviated from the majority of its suffering (though no such thing is possible) will soon be alleviated from its religion as well. This is primarily what accounts for the commoners move away from organized religion.

56

The most evident example of mankind's vanity can be found in his belief in God. God did not create man in His own image any more than He modeled the platypus after Himself.

57

A soldier of God? Can there be no greater coward that he?

58

To lament the loss of the blessed Garden of Eden is a thinly-veiled desire to have never been born.

59

Those who would think their fate less miserable and their life more tolerable in the kingdom of heaven would find that they are as equally unsatisfied to exist there as well.

60

The man who seeks to be spiritually "saved" is often immature in character, else he would have already rescued himself.

61

Beware the man who does not bubble with humor, even in the most dire of circumstances, for he is more demon than any that has ever been previously described by man.

62

What I would not tolerate from any man, I would not stand from God as well.

63

"God" is the collective intellect of mankind, which appears to be regressing with each new generation.

64

As science began to rule, man became somewhat detached from his poetic relationship to the cosmos — the poetic imagination that religion once provided to the exclusion of reason. Nowadays a man chooses to take sides, either to be religious or scientific. Yet any man, if he is to truly develop his character sufficiently, must be intimately acquainted with both poetry and science.

65

To ask of purity from man is to ask the impossible. We should be so lucky to settle for his refinement.

66

Hope, without resolve and action, is a child merely dreaming.

67

The idea expressed in the example of Job isn't some inane lesson about subservience. Job is not demonstrating his loyalty to a spiteful and cruel entity in the sky but to an idea — the idea that what is most important in life isn't one's possessions, family, accomplishments, or health, but the contemplation of the value that each of these may hold — a reflection often only perceived through the lens of some tragedy.

68

In his depiction of God — the morality of God, the character of God — man proves himself to be a brute once again.

69

It's better to do away with the notion of a personal "God" forevermore and refer to the idea as Being.

70

Those whose mission it is to denigrate science for the benefit of their own personal, sacred beliefs would seek to discard some of mankind's greatest accomplishments for the comfort of his most cherished lies.

71

If you must imagine an all seeing, all knowing set of eyes upon you — judging all that you do — in order to do what you know in your heart to be true and just and decent — imagine those eyes to be your own.

72

The religious man has all the faith in the world in the science of his time, enjoying the luxuries and benefits of its practice, except when it fails to endorse his prejudices.

73

Mankind peers into the sublime complexity of the universe and fails to experience the divine, so he invents a God instead.

74

The religious man's apparent disdain for sensuality is, in reality, the sensually pleasurable experience of self-denial and self-torture.

75

The man who chooses to reject the truth because its result would be unsettling makes of cowardice a kind of virtue.

76

As the religious man imagines himself connected to the divine power of the invisible realm, the man of wealth believes himself connected to the divine realm of the physical. Both are disconnected from the only true source of "divinity," that which arises from within and grounds a man in both the physical and the imaginative. This is the power that one must learn to tap in order to truly live a spiritual life.

77

The devil is only considered as the antithesis to the divine because he refused to acknowledge man as something worthy of admiration.

78

Mankind *imagines* that there is a God, but he should *know* there is not.

79

There is a newer, sicker version of Christianity enveloping the Western world — that of a dogmatic homogeny; an ideal of the human being as an antiseptic embodiment of a neutral Christ.

80

There is no God amidst an empty church except perhaps left there as a painting or some other work of art. A God only exists among a certain populace. He appears as an infant, an old man, a young woman, and a dog on the street. The wrath of God represented in their hatreds, their desires, and their fears; the beauty of a God in their creations, their kindness, and their tears. While the wrath of God may be confused for evil, more often than not it is simply man's own fear refusing to believe that beauty can be sublime and the truth so painful. If the church is evil, it is man who has made it so.

81

If everyone living could be convinced that there is no God, it may be true, given man's dependence, that there would ensue chaos in the streets; however, such a riot need not have been necessary. God is a crutch for the fool who doesn't realize that he can walk erect.

82

Religion does not raise a man atop a mountain peak so that he may look down. Rather it keeps him upon the ground looking up.

83

One interpretation of the Holy Scriptures is to understand that any use of the Lord's name is to use it vainly. "God" is the ultimate vulgarity. Thus, the scriptures themselves are, in a sense, vulgar in that they cannot possibly describe and define accurately that which is beyond description and definition. Instead, they are merely one early attempt to give voice to something that a man feels deeply within, an understanding of the universe that is essentially poetic and ultimately beyond the reach of words. All works of art have this as their conscious or unconscious aim, to express some aspect of that unspeakable abyss that we can only address with the word "divine." A church then, if one is necessary, should be a place where men go to congregate in discussion about a variety of works of art rather than merely one.

84

"God" is an entity that should be conceived only in the manger of one's own imagination and worshipped only in the church of one's own heart.

85

Organized religion is merely the gathering together of uninspired souls — men of little imagination or spirit. They are the accountants and doctors whose professions were chosen for their expedience; the fanatically fearful parents; the dry and dispossessed professors who no longer recall their original enthusiasm for all things noble and great; those too old to remember life; those too young to have lived it; those unfortunate souls who have been either blessed with little in the way of talent and/or capacity or beaten down by circumstance; the chaste librarians; remorseful criminals; and drunkards who wish to sober themselves — a whole congregation of lotus-eaters who hope to escape the pain of life through delusion.

86

The great and noble king has hired a fool to be his interpreter. Essentially, this is the problem of religion as a whole.

87

It is precisely those concrete thinkers who cannot comprehend the invariables of abstract thought — the uncertainties of existence — who seek refuge in religion.

88

The man who thinks that he is Christ has more merit than the man who simply believes in him.

89

The saying, "there but for the grace of God go I" implies that in the other case, God is graceless. This is always true of the "other" in religion.

90

Even if there were a chance that the devout Christians were indeed correct about their understanding of heaven, then hell would be a small price to pay in order to avoid contact with them.

91

God, too, is an idea and "His" thoughts are in reality the expression of mankind's silent meditations.

92

For those who *need* a God or unifying narrative, but have matured enough that you can no longer tolerate the children's stories that dominate the landscape of "wisdom" literature, I suggest you begin to think of Nature as some kind of deity, though hardly a personal one. She can be thought of rather as an organizing force that seeks to maintain equilibrium within her realm, visiting either good or evil on he that disturbs the harmony. Her only commandment, since she is beyond the scope of moral judgment, being unconscious, is: "Thou shalt not upset the balance." This idea, of course, will certainly upset the lotus-eaters, being as they are chained to their deluded and egotistical idea that they possess some kind of value as an individual even though they can only properly function among the herd. Indeed their small modicum of individuality is the reason *for* their suffering. Regardless, Nature can serve as an example for the more mature man to follow. He, too, needs to create balance in his own life through the means of moderation and contemplation. And if his ego still twinges from time to time, he may think of himself as Nature's consciousness, the only means she has to experience and reflect upon herself.

93

Religion is nothing more nor less than a failed philosophical theory (as all such theories are). It is a "failure" in the sense that it cannot logically purport to be the expression of one great overall truth. It is merely something which may stimulate the contemplation of man and bring him closer to an understanding of himself and the universe. Any particular work of religion is just one in a great many "sacred" texts that may aid man with the development of his character.

94

The devoutly religious man mostly seems to be lacking the element of spirituality that he adamantly professes his religion has given him. He appears as something of a naturalistic painting of a tree that is missing the most essential element that would otherwise animate it with life.

95

"God" arrives only if a man can come to accept that there is no God.

96

The religious man does not pray for peace, but victory.

97

The Gods of "civilized" man always seem to be aggrandizements of him.

98

The truly spiritual man serves the will of "God" though he has never believed in Him.

99

The religious man has the same solution to the problem of death as does the mortician, a smiling corpse.

100

Every time a church bell rings, one can hear the screams of the dying souls inside.

101

How so much purity seems to drip from the whore after bathing.

102

The problem with the "God" of organized religion is that man finds a deity that is morally not much better than himself, sometimes much worse.

103

The "miracle" of Christ was in his character, not his resurrection. Only the fools of spectacle needed such an ostentatious and miraculous show, so they created it themselves.

104

"God" is merely an object of religious feeling, not an entity in itself. It is the feeling that is real, inspired by a myriad of experiences — the most universal of which is nature — and hardly subject to religious laws, dogma, or tradition.

105

You can be reasonably sure that you are championing the morally righteous cause if the religious men are in the majority against you.

106

Man did not become victorious over death by the creation of his religions, he merely pretended that it were so — a childish game for childish souls.

107

To witness a child ripped from its mother's breast by death or, worse yet, the death of a mother who leaves behind the child, alone in the world without the comfort of its wellspring, is more than enough to unequivocally prove that a personal, just, and reasonable "God" is nothing but a fiction. There can be no satisfactory reason, however so divine, to elicit justice from such a state of affairs. The mind of man may be limited, but he can recognize the fundamental flaw in any attempt to justify the actions of a "reasonable God" in these circumstances. It defies reason precisely because it *is* unreasonable. Likewise, a personal "God" would suggest that "He" have some concern for the individual under "His" watch and care, yet these scenarios, and there are many others more striking and terrible, imply a decided lack of concern on the part of the deity. Only the most heartless of fathers would subject their children to the kind of hardships, sufferings, and horrors that "God" provides for "His" so that they might earn a place beside "Him." It is an inferior interpretation of a work of art.

108

A man takes more care of those things he values but fears to lose than those that he possesses but believes he will forever retain. Thus, he should minister to his life and soul with more significance and treat them both with the utmost care, being sure to give them both his full and undivided attention. Yet, more often than not, he would rather tend to the childish fantasy of eternal life and immortality.

109

There is nothing sadder than the dying of a child, especially if it is made to suffer, nothing more unjust and despicable, nothing more hateful and unforgiving. Any conception of some personal God that would allow such a thing to occur, for whatever reason, must be denounced immediately as something of a demon, an uncaring egotist who merely wishes to flaunt His powers on earth and boast that He possesses some larger plan for the universe. Yet, no such God has ever existed that would be so cruel and unconcerned. Instead, it reflects the nature of the artists who created such a God. They, being almost wholly untroubled by reason, were a fearful and somewhat diminutive people and can be forgiven (to a certain degree) for the flaws inherent in their storytelling. In the modern age, however, there are more apologists for this type of God than there are true believers. This is because they so desire a personal relationship with the universe which has no concern for them at all. They still remain frightened and tearful children.

110

There are two kinds of truths in the world — factual truth and artistic truth. Organized religion does not merely confuse the two. Instead, it attempts to merge them together into one because the devotedly religious man is incapable of comprehending truth that is artistic and abstract — no doubt because these are either too confusing to him or he is unwilling to exert the necessary effort to understand.

111

Love did not "transform the world," as the Christians often claim. There are just as many nations who despise and attempt to eradicate their neighbors as there were in the time of antiquity. The Greeks readily discussed the power of Eros long before the idea of Christ was introduced into the world. Perhaps it is true that there are more men now who *talk* of love and bandy the word about as if it were some sort of magical talisman; however, there are no more men who *feel* love today than there were in the era of the pre-Christian. The Christian idea of love did not transform the world as much as it helped create yet another lie by which men might continue to delude themselves — a necessary lie, to be sure, given the ferocity and beastliness of mankind's potential, but a lie nonetheless.

112

The "let's all just love one another" utopian mentality of the religious romantic ignores the necessity of conflict and suffering for both the betterment of the individual and the impetus to spark the creative.

88

Nevertheless, it asks the impossible of a man and is an insufficient and childish answer to the problem of war, totalitarianism, and destruction.

113

The lion has no natural desire to lie with the lamb, nor the lamb to snuggle with the lion. These are the daydreams of an inferior consciousness that seeks to impose a more desirable order on the world, but one which is only organic to the abstract realm man's imagination.

114

The Christian is instructed to put away all childish things when he becomes a man except the religion itself, thus insuring that he will never truly rise to maturity.

115

The only ideas which are not worthy of tolerance are those which reek of certainty, and even they must merely face the threat of ridicule and derision   unless they seek to take up arms.

116

A traditional and well established religious perspective is an absolute necessity for the vast majority of men who, without it, would engage in even worst atrocities than those they have rained down upon the earth in the name of some particular God. Such men simply cannot breathe the rarified air of enlightenment unless it be filtered through the screen of an organized religious understanding. Without the simplified justifications for a higher moral order and purpose to the universe, the common man will quickly fall into vice and his society will revert to chaos.

117

Most believe that with responsibility and sacrifice comes maturity, but these do little to subdue a man's youthful and fickle passions. Responsibility might make him more subservient to be sure, yet the child will still seethe beneath the mask that he has been made to wear.

118

Man seems to have unbounded hope for the new generation though it is to be raised and brought to "adulthood" by the old. This is the vicious circle of "manhood."

119

Even rebellion has been made chic, welcomed into the company of fools. The rebel of today has nothing to say, only the desire to rebuke authority — a childish exploit that epitomizes what has become of this childish creature known as man.

120

The young at heart are too often young in mind as well.

121

The Romantics and the Christians all point to the child and applaud its innocent, free spirit. The Romantics perceive the child as uninhibited and free from the annoyances of society. The Christians view a creature that is not burdened by the truths of the world, the evils and the various acts of corrupted spirit. Yet, both sentimentalize youth as if these were the only characteristics of the young. The Christian, obviously, adores purity and ignorance. Yet, he ignores the viciousness in the child that is in need of sublimation and outright scorns the curiosity of the child that seeks to transcend his ignorance. The Romantic, looking into himself and deploring his own conformity, sighs longingly about his youth and forgets its main tenet of dependence. The child is free only insofar as others allow him to be. If left to himself he would surely perish within the week. He is dependent on others to provide him the freedom that the Romantic so desires. The child is in a constant fight for independence — as too should be the man.

122

The passion of youth bursts forth sparks from its fire, but it is an uncontrolled and therefore only tangentially worthwhile burn. Their passion is admirable, but its untamed nature makes it dangerous and not particularly useful to both the person and the world.

123

Mankind spends far too much time in the attempt to tame nature and not nearly enough time taming himself — the only creature of earth that has any need of taming. The trick, of course, is to tame a man without making of him a docile, pampered, and conquered thing.

124

Maturity does not consist of undertaking more complex responsibilities but in understanding more complex perspectives.

125

Maturity is simply a higher state of awareness.

126

Maturity too often peaks well before one's death — sometimes as an unfortunate result of infirmity, but usually by choice. Thus begins what some refer to as a second childhood.

127

Self-control is a necessary, though hardly sufficient, component of maturity.

128

The child does not recognize that the monster in his closet is him.

129

Mankind seems intent on glorifying the worst aspects of childhood while disregarding its best as something childish.

130

Ask nothing of the young for they are sure to tell you everything that they know.

131

Man seems to often make the wrong choice defiantly, as a child rebelling against its parent. He should be inwardly cognizant of the proper path, but he inevitably chooses the wrong one. Perhaps he does this for the experience, a chance for comparison. Perhaps it is ego or deaf pride. Or perhaps he is simply a child who has yet to mature.

132

Pay little attention to the words of the young and smile sweetly while they rant. For they will awaken one day to the embarrassment that they ever opened their mouths. Unless, of course, they fail to mature. Then they will merely grow louder.

133

There is little more pathetic than an old man devoid of wisdom, still clinging to the notions of his youth, still believing in the magical properties of unicorns and fairies. His only wish being that he should be young again.

134

It is possible to distract yourself to such a degree that you are similar to the child who enters a movie theatre and emerges seventy years later to find himself an old man, none the wiser for the experience.

135

No man should fashion an opinion who hasn't first heard and sought to understand a good many other opinions from a variety of significant sources — thus the reason why no one should pay much attention to the ramblings of the young. Their entire system of knowledge is merely a knee-jerk reaction to the superficial offerings of their narrow world. A temporary incest of the mind occurs that can produce dull, slow witted children not much different from their source — temporary, of course, only insofar that these youths venture out into the world to experience and wrestle with the great minds of the present and the past. The rest will wallow in the shallowness of youth forevermore.

136

It should trouble man more that he confers the weaponry of power into the hands of those who still defiantly profess to believe in Santa Claus.

92

137

The majority can never be expected to make a choice for their own overall benefit. They are like children locked in a room full of vegetables and candy.

138

Prejudices of youth and understanding (the foundations for all prejudice) should be naturally overcome with age and the accumulation of varied experiences — unless, of course, one proceeds to cultivate provincialism and immaturity. Then will one's prejudices become solidified until such a time that one either matures or begins to encounter and confront a wider world.

139

Morality is not simply a social fiction but is something deeply felt by everyone — a sense of fairness. The child first feels it whenever things don't progress to his advantage. Everything is unfair to him that does not suit his wants and needs at the moment. If properly cultivated, this perception of fairness will later include the wants and needs of others as well. While politeness and manners are entirely superficial, they serve to provide an expression for the child's innate sense of justice. What began with a declaration of "I want" transforms to the idea of "I deserve."

140

The well-bred child who is poorly raised, by himself as well as his parents, will turn out more deficient in character than will the one whose circumstances are the reverse.

141

The Marquis de Sade was not mad after all. He merely refused to relinquish his childhood to maturity. For that, he became the hero of immature souls everywhere.

142

The repressive conservative often believes himself to be the most mature because externally he seems to have put away all his "childish things." Yet, his spirit is often the most childish of all. The best things of childhood he *has* abandoned — curiosity, imagination, awe and passion — while retaining the child's propensity for being small minded, arrogant, and too readily agreeable.

143

There are two different types of maturity. There is intellectual maturity and emotional maturity. The latter will sometimes arise with age while the former may never come to be at all. The problem is that the majority of men lack both.

144

The old man who envies the youth their pleasures suffers from a rather common torment of age; that is, he has failed to cultivate the more sophisticated, subtle, and noble pleasures that arise from experience and care. In other words, he is still a child in many important ways.

145

The religious law and the law of the state exist for the same reason: they each have no trust that mankind as a whole is capable of knowing and doing what should be done in any particular situation.

146

The religious life is not a virtuous one in and of itself. Instead of a living work of art, it has become instead an accumulation of particular customs taught to children in order to practice their own moral instruction. These habits, however, quickly become something considered divine in themselves — thus transforming religion into something of a facade of virtue.

147

If you take away a people's religion, at least with respect to those poor, lesser souls who so densely populate the earth, you take away their ability to "self"-govern as well. They possess no inherent skill at governing themselves, lacking as they are in prudence, patience, or tolerance, so a codified book of moral laws is necessary.

148

Man is not born with some original sin hanging over his head, but neither is he born as some saintly angel — pure and perfect in his innocence. Instead, each child is born with a distinctive character in need of cultivation. The means by which to foster the child will be dependent upon his personality. The man of brawn and action, for instance, will have little need for books but he will need to be introduced to the concepts of fairness and civility lest he be tempted to use his strength for something ill. Both the genetics of nature and the nurture of environment are involved in the raising of a mature man. Yet, it is likely that he will be born deficient in both. Thus the need for cultivation.

149

In order to even attempt religion, one must become a kind of scholar first, with a curious eye trained on a variety of textual intricacies and profundities from a vast array of literature in the hope of eking out wisdom and truth, even if it be of an abstract or metaphoric understanding.

150

To misinterpret a verse of poetry is worse than not being able to read the verse at all since in the latter case a man will remain at least somewhat contrite because he is more than aware of his inadequacies while the former believes that he is in possession of truth.

151

The majority of men do not understand their religion, although they can perform it. Without ritual and a rather simple-minded focus on merely one particular text, the average man would have no means to consciously participate, albeit superficially, in the divine.

152

Religion is not the opiate of the masses, as Marx romantically muses. It is, instead, essential to the general well being of the common man, ill-equipped as he is, despite Marx's faith in him, at mastering the difficult task of understanding.

153

The "religion" of the Metaphorist is similar to Judaism in that its focus is on a close study of the holy texts, excepting that the definition of a sacred text for the Metaphorist includes any material that might provide for a deeper understanding of the world or oneself. Unlike the established ancient religions, however, the Metaphorist interprets all sacred works as pieces of art with symbolic, instead of literal, significance. In this manner, the Metaphoristic approach is more fluid and variable with the possibility for the acceptance of a multiplicity of interpretations — the best being whichever provides the most profound significance for the life of any one particular individual at any one particular time. The disadvantage of this method, of course, is that it admits to no certainty whatsoever. Interpretations are drawn using textual evidence, creativity, and intelligence, as well as one's own experience and prior knowledge. Thus, not merely *any* interpretation will suffice, yet most men will feel uncomfortable with a variety of perfectly legitimate perspectives which may change over time instead of the familiarity of one definitive and changeless understanding. Additionally, the Metaphoristic technique demands a great deal of effort. After all, there is no list of sanctified texts, paintings, or music. A man must utilize the experience of others to introduce him to these works in his youth, presumably through education, and then work diligently for the rest of his days to expand his spirit through this kind of encounter with art. Finally, the definition of a "sacred" work is inherently vague. If the Metaphoristic definition of a "sacred" text includes any material that might provide for a deeper understanding of the world or oneself, then this allows for anything whatsoever to be considered as something holy, which renders the word itself meaningless. These are some of the difficulties inherent in the "religion" of the Metaphorist. Perhaps these challenges explain why only the very few will ever dare to practice it.

154

The followers of Christ abandon or betray him at his most crucial hour, the time of his arrest. It is the shame of their desertion which induces them to "see" Christ rise from the grave. Their delusion serves to excuse and justify their actions while assuaging their profound sense of guilt and inadequacy. Most of the institutionalized religions have this same element of self-loathing to them.

155

The true beauty of Christ is eclipsed by his resurrection.

156

That which seems to be a devil at first glance often arrives as an angel in disguise. The reverse is likewise true.

157

The religious man, who insists that he would have a better life as a believer even if it turns out in the end that there is no God, is similar to the man who chooses to ingest a pill that alters his perception of reality to such a degree that he no longer is able to discern it from illusion. In fact, he rationalizes that since the illusion is more fulfilling to him than the truth, it is also more profound.

158

Each man must make for himself his own religion, fashioned upon the designs of his better self.

159

A man is only separated from God insofar as he is alienated from himself.

160

Faith in one's projects should replace one's faith in God. The first demonstrates a confidence in oneself while the second betrays a lack of it.

161

Sola Scriptura is the Latin phrase that literally means "by scripture alone," which gave the Protestant Christian believer unmitigated access to the mind of the divine through individual study of the Bible itself. Yet, providing access to the divine is true of a great deal of other literature as well. In fact, this is the intention of all true art — to provide a glimpse into the divine nature of the universe. Thus, to be well read is to be connected to the divine. Of course, in order to accomplish such a feat, a man must also learn to read well.

162

The rabid fool who burns books because he is offended by the ideas in them is no less cowardly and fanatical in his own beliefs than those ideas which he is protesting. It is often the fanatic who, prejudicially, ignorantly, and without a hint of self-awareness, becomes the easiest to offend because of his own feverous devotion to a perspective that is simultaneously self-righteous and does not allow for adaptation to a changing world. The fanatic embraces simple answers to complex questions and believes himself to be somewhat wise for the accomplishment. However, his significant lack of insight, intelligence, and intuition make him little more than a ranting child who has not yet learned the virtue of prudence, but for whom pride is an all consuming panacea to his own shortcomings as a human being.

163

It is possible, as well as enviable, to be wild in spirit while simultaneously domesticated in action.

7

The State of Morality and Ethics

1

The true ethical question is not, as Kant suggests, should my maxim be a universal law, but would I honestly still act in a similar manner or perform a similar deed if the entire world should truly know of it and my intentions?

2

Only fools believe that because morality has no universal foundation, that is, it isn't rooted in some timeless precondition that exists beyond the human, that it necessarily has no meaning or no ground which requires a person to respect its principles. This is only due to the fact that reason has become a kind of Old Testament God. If one cannot find a reasonable justification for something, then it is thought to lack validity. If that were so, then love would possess little meaning whatsoever. Morality has always been relative. It has been the shared beliefs in certain aspects of the moral that has kept morality from being the kind of relative "free for all" that so scares the lotus-eaters. After all, people cannot help but share certain moral beliefs in common due to the commonality of their sentiments. If nothing else, a man has his own sense of moral intuition that can ground him, imperfect though it may be.

2

Man is usually the politician for morality and rarely its ambassador.

3

A man's response to what he views as an atrocity is more a product of his culture than it is his morality.

4

A kind of blind self-interest permeates all of morality. Yet, while we may wish for a man's intentions to be pure, the fact that he is self-interested does not make him less moral. Morality and mankind are both too complex to bow before such simplistic and childish concepts as selflessness and purity. How might we possibly know a man's intentions? How might he? And why should we suspect that they are reducible to any single motivation, stripped of all complexity?

5

If man were somehow fundamentally moral, there would be no need for law. Yet, the laws of the state are essential for men to live among one another. He must also be curbed by the judgment of his neighbors who carry out the unwritten laws, the breaking of which result in censure and banishment. These more subtle laws, too, must be enforced to rein the yearnings of the man-child lest his inner nature get the better of him. Often these laws are the more troubling for a man. He simply cannot stand to be censured in such an isolating manner, unified as he is to the mob. The greater man has no need for such restraints once he has matured.

6

Morality is sometimes nothing more than a social fiction designed to maximize group cohesion. It is precisely these laws which often change over time.

7

How many would successfully pass the test offered by Socrates with the ring of Gyges? How many would remain moral without the repercussion of consequences? Of those who believe they would, how many would do so without the guarantee that others would become aware that they indeed passed the test? How many are lying to yourself?

8

Hate is a weapon wielded by the weak of mind and soul.

9

If you offer up the other cheek to your enemy, you should not be surprised that he hits you again.

10

Vengeance is the child's reaction to injustice.

11

Moral reasoning is the rational mind of man trying to rationally justify what his intuitions have already decided.

12

Kant's desire to elicit standards of behavior based upon whether one can logically wish for a maxim to apply to everyone is contrived to fit the rigid understanding of logic. Yet, it is not logical to assume that any maxim will obtain to everyone at any given time. It may seem logical to assert that lying is wrong because I wouldn't want others to lie to me and that lying itself would make the very possibility of truth telling irrelevant. Yet, since I know that not everyone will adopt my maxim to lie when I wish to gain a particular advantage, I am free to practice the principle as long as I remain undetected. Of course, I fail to respect the rational agency of a person in such a case, but I both deny that rational agency is anything worthy of such exalted respect to the extent that Kant demands and that the majority of men possess respectable rational agency to the extent that they deserve my unearned respect.

13

Morality is often immediately discarded at the moment when it is no longer perceived to be in one's own self-interest.

14

It is impossible to refrain from ever doing injustice to another, though perhaps worthy of effort at times. The worthier goal, however, is to not do injustice to oneself. The more one honestly succeeds at the latter, the less likely it will be for one to commit the former.

15

The man without mercy is of that particular breed of human who rates beneath the animal.

16

The cause and therefore the cure for injustice lies in the hearts and minds of men.

17

To the young child justice is simply the attainment of what he wants and injustice is when he is thwarted in the attempt. This is the notion of justice at its most elemental level. You don't then have to teach a child the truth about justice; you instead make him aware of the complexities of the idea and the consequences of his overt selfishness. The difficulty, of course, is that if a just action cannot be reconciled with a man's own selfish wants and desires, it never *feels* like justice.

18

Morality doesn't make mankind any more divine than does the speed of the cheetah or the eyesight of the eagle allocate them for any kind of special consideration.

19

Aristotle writes that a man needs more than just an understanding or insight into justice. In order to be just one must also perform just actions. Thus, one can conceivably cultivate justice in one's heart through habitually practicing justice. Yet, it's important to add that the action itself does not necessarily correspond to the state of being "just." Let us say that I understand the nature of justice and I perform an action that is just. However, I only intend to perform such an act in order that others will praise me for my deed, not because I am truly a just person. I don't *become* just by my action, I am merely being judged to be so by others who assume my inner intentions were just as well. Yet only I can ever truly know whether I am morally commendable or not. Men often mistake each other for possessing good character when, in fact, they are more often simply giving show to their vanity. Men, too, often mistake themselves for possessing good character because they look only at their actions and conveniently neglect that which they should know to be true in their hearts; that is, if they were capable of being honest with themselves.

20

The whore who labors only part of her day in order to lift her to something greater will use that remaining time hosing herself off in some fashion. The same is true of lies.

21

The ethics of an "eye for an eye" mentality does little to enhance the vision of anyone.

22

There exists no man that is amoral. There may be some men whose moral universe is in complete contrast to that of his contemporaries, but man cannot possibly prevent himself from judging things from a moral perspective. He is, after all, not capable of relinquishing his attachment to certain things and his revulsion of others which is the very basis of morality.

23

The primary thing that scientific experimentation on animals continues to prove is that man has climbed to his position at the top of the food chain by demonstrating his capacity for superior brutality and self-righteous justification. He judges nature to be immoral, yet shows nothing better of himself.

24

A righteous man will one day come to notice that there are others in the world who are not so. No doubt he will make this assessment in his youth and he will be tempted by the impetuousness of his age to desire the elimination of these unrighteous souls in order to rid the world of their kind. Yet, if he is to eventually mature and become a thoughtful and noble man, he will soon realize that at the moment he should attempt to eradicate even a single unworthy fool from existence, he loses his claim to his righteousness and becomes something no more worthy than they. His righteousness, it seems, is more of a burden than a privilege

25

Cursed be the soul that would charge another with moral crimes festering in his own untended mind.

26

Nietzsche's idea that man should undertake a "revaluation of all values" is an individual undertaking. It cannot be a process embarked upon by the collective, especially the political, mind as the collective is only concerned with its own needs as a whole and will, no doubt, ignore what the individual requires for his own life.

27

Modern man seems to have eliminated shame from his experience. The religious man of the past seemed to be shameful of everything, but modern man possesses little shame at all. In fact, he views his shamelessness as a virtue, a type of bravery in which a man refuses to apologize for being who he is. His lack of shame, he thinks, is a kind of supreme and faithful individuality that admits to no fault so egregious that should cause him to feel regret. Shame, for him, is merely a label that originates outside himself and is forced upon him by others. It is they who judge his actions shameful rather than the actions being so in and of themselves. In this regard he has no interest in acting with any other kind of integrity or virtue other than that of his own desire to express himself as he sees fit to do. Yet, shame is often an invaluable aid to the development of one's character, serving as it does to rein a man to his limitations lest he fly too closely to the sun. In fact, modern man, above all, has a great deal of which he *should* be ashamed.

28

The philosopher laments that there is no grounding to ethics without God. Yet, as Hume realized, ethics are grounded in human sentiments which is something more substantial than simply personal choice. Kindness is not an ethical virtue because God says that it is so, but because man feels it to be intuitively essential — perhaps primarily because he would like it reflected back to him.

29

The difficulty, of course, of grounding ethics within human sentiments is that oftentimes men are wrong with respect to their intuitions and deluded about their motives or desires. Thus, the need for a man to be the most honest with himself and develop within the virtue of wisdom so that he might be able to decipher whether his sentiments are driven by some sort of pathetic repression or an overdeveloped attachment to tradition. Such wisdom will require him to study a variety of different sources from art, philosophy, science, history, and religion. Therefore, it will require a man of special character.

30

The evils of man are always the result of some faulty perception that he has accepted as true. If you wish to abolish the evil within him, you must first find a way to alter this perception.

31

Man has made a slave of nature all around him which, if he does not quickly free, will result in a terrifying revolt.

32

The man who thinks of morality as something simple and innate, a kind of heightened common sense, understands it, quite simply, not at all. In fact, the more complex the system, the more often one's common instinct is wrong about it.

33

The only person a man should never lie to is himself, developing the kind of character that is able to withstand the harsh and brutal facts of his existence. Yet, don't expect this same brand of inner strength in other men who, for the most part, must be indulged with certain falsehoods like children until they have proven themselves to be mature.

34

To forgive the extreme stupidities of man is to tacitly consent to their effects. Forgiveness in these cases should only be granted to those who have made some kind of effort to undo the consequences of their stupidity.

35

It is impossible for a man to *truly* love his neighbors. The best that one may ask of him is to tolerate them for his own sake. A love so broadly construed as to include all of humanity is one which is lacking in profundity and depth and betrays a certain poverty of understanding.

36

In one sense everything *is* permitted and there exists no morality in nature that dictates that man should act in any other way than what suits him. The universe will not so much as shrug the eradication of mankind no matter what means are used to dispose of him. In another sense, man sets his own restrictions based upon the limitations which exist within him — limitations which, if he would take the time to look, he will find himself sorely lacking.

37

"I am limitless!" cries Icarus just before his plunge into the sea.

38

There are many who will berate a man for his lack of overwhelming love of humanity or his refusal to grant mankind a special pardon because of the accomplishments of those few spirits who were not as ignorant, callous, banal, stupid, and brutal as the remainder of humanity. These are the apologists of man who fail to acknowledge the gross inadequacies of themselves and their fellows and, instead, extol the virtues of the anomalies. The effect is an over-evaluation of the species and an egotistical and undeserved estimation of oneself.

39

Men more often develop principles so that they might show them off to their neighbors and brag that theirs are more virtuous than others — clawing, killing, and overpowering one another over ideologies, principles, and morality that they themselves do not even follow in practice.

40

A man who is quick to take offense is often the same man who is even quicker to give it.

41

Man congratulates himself for his moral goodness because he extends a hand to his fellow man in brotherhood. Yet, this act is more often than not a social conceit that is offered only to those who are most similar to members of his own tribe, in other words, to those whom he considers related to him — to his brothers. Moral praise, however, should not be bestowed upon a man because he shows affection for a member of his family (even if that family includes all of humanity). It's natural that he should do so. Evolution demands it of him.

42

The force that leads a man to the gas chamber, or any other of the thousands of unspeakable horrors inflicted upon humanity by itself, is the unquestionable certainty of a man's perspective.

43

My harsh critique of man, at least the majority of men, is not a call for his extermination but a cry for him to elevate himself. Those who are troubled by any sort of rank attributed to a man as something leading to a mass eradication of those "lesser" souls have already conceded my assessment of man's predilection for brutality by the mere presence of their trepidation.

44

The hedonist betrays a significant lack of character primarily because of his childish concern for little but himself. In his search for pleasuring himself, he gives only the slightest thought as to how his actions might affect those around him or the environment in general. He gives only a sideward glance to future generations, whether his own or those of his neighbor, and goes about his day as if the universe will end at the moment of his demise. While he does not, to his credit, accept the delusions of grandeur propagated by the cult of immortality, neither does he assume responsibility for anything other than himself ultimately.

45

A man gains nothing at all from flatterers except to obtain a chorus of souls who are willing to sing the praises of his name on the mountaintop. Yet, such a man as he who would desire such a collection of fools around him is usually in no need of other means to exalt his name. His own inflated ego will often serve him quite well.

46

With respect to virtues, every man possesses all of them while simultaneously possessing none. Their presence or absence at any particular time is often determined by the choice one makes in a situation which calls for the employment of a virtue. Wisdom, then, is the highest virtue since it reigns over all the others in determining the proper choice for any particular course of action. Sadly, it is the virtue that is quite noticeably lacking in the vast majority of men because they either spend so little time cultivating it or they fail to recognize its presence and authority, often mistaking it for the commonsensical folk-wisdom of their similarly wayward forefathers.

47

A man should examine and correct his own faults before he feels it necessary to correct the faults of another. This task alone should keep him sufficiently occupied so that he never has the occasion to point his finger in the direction of another man. The development of his character is all that should concern him.

48

The man who tolerates everything, the poor naïve and "open minded" fool, lives with little to no morality at all, while the man who tolerates little in life is too much of a moralist, believing black and white to be the only gradations of color in the world. If one were forced to choose one above the other, the former is more interesting and lively.

49

It would seem that the rough beast of Yeats' poetic vision, who slouches toward Bethlehem to be born again, is man himself — ignorant, lazy, well fed, certain of himself, and indifferent to the concerns of other creatures almost altogether.

50

A man is born neither good nor bad, neither virtuous nor riddled with vice. Instead he acquires these qualities or discards them as he sees fit. He does this through a series of choices that vary by their degree of intensity and import, yet which often are made without much reflection and a great deal of them are chosen almost absent-mindedly. This gives the impression that his choices were not freely chosen; however, the man himself is responsible for his lack of awareness. He has chosen his ignorance in that he has done nothing to alleviate it and his decision to act unreflectively is a particular perspective that he has adopted into his lifestyle. He celebrates it each time he reflexively responds to stimuli that might have otherwise been approached reflectively.

51

The fundamentalist suffers from a premature shuttering of his moral education. He was provided the early portion of his training, that which armed him with specific, absolute rules, the kind of simple directives which are given to most children — never hit, steal, lie, or otherwise hurt another person. Yet, his education was abandoned at this point, for whatever reason, and he never learned the more subtle and sophisticated skills of reflection and scrutiny which might have otherwise led him to an understanding of the malleable nature of morality.

52

The only thing truly worthwhile in the vast collection of Aristotle's work is his book on Ethics, by far the best treatise on how a man should go about living the best life possible. It makes the moral pronouncements of religion seem shrill, unlearned, and ridiculous by comparison.

53

Given the absence of universal moral law, man has the freedom to act in any way that he wishes without fear of some kind of divine retribution. However, one must still face the retribution of man, which is in every way just as cruel, fierce, and unrelenting as the wrath of God.

54

The brute criminal demonstrates an immorality operating primarily on a physical level whereas the more insidious evil of fundamentalism functions at the level of the spirit. The former destroys the body while the latter destroys the soul.

55

There are a great many crimes to humanity which do not include violence and death.

56

As with all things related to ethics, justice does not exist within the world itself, but as something which mankind brings to the world. It exists only insofar as he exists. Yet, for the majority of men, justice is nothing more than childish retribution. They are unable or unwilling to perceive of justice as anything more nuanced and complex than as an instrument for personal vengeance.

57

It is the immature mind that seeks some kind of ultimate —perfect — justice.

58

The evolution of morality, that process by which man becomes more humane and less of a brute, requires first an act of rebellion — someone must venture forth and break the moral law in some fashion before morality itself can loosen the lines that moor it to tradition. Otherwise, the majority of nations would still be stoning their citizens and crucifying their criminals. The true rebel, then, should be seated at a place of high honor in any society that hopes to improve upon itself.

59

A man develops a moral identity in the same way that he creates a personal identity — though practice, reflection, repetition, and experience.

60

The difficulty of ethical behavior for a man is that he finds it extremely demanding of his time, effort, and attention. He finds it much easier to rationalize and lie to himself about the content of his character.

61

There exists no such thing as color except through the perception allowed by the human eye. So, it has no universal foundation in the world other than man himself. Yet, a man would not concede that color does not exist for him in any significant way. The same is true of morality, although for *that* a man requires that there be some sort of foundational tie to the natural world in order to have meaning — forgetting, of course, that *he* is a part of nature.

62

The only real difference between the modern conception of the death penalty and the drawing and quartering of criminals is that the latter example is more honest. The former attempts to make the procedure more "humane" by making it more sterile and moving it away from the public streets. The effect, of course, is a procedure that is certainly less painful and bloody. The cruelty and ignorance, however, remain.

63

Freedom from responsibility is a childish notion — a desire to be unburdened of the pressures to conform to the rules and dictates of a society that man himself created, untroubled by uncertainty, and unbothered by the implications of his actions. In fact, freedom itself is a great responsibility since abuse of it will ultimately lead a man to ruin. Freedom, therefore, must be used wisely and thoughtfully. Most men today who talk of freedom usually desire liberty from duty, obligation, and commitment.

64

To sympathize with the stupid man, the unwise man, is to tacitly accept that he has no choice in his decision — that he is merely at the mercy of forces beyond his control and understanding. Yet, as Sartre claimed, this state of being is a choice that such a man has made — either in his youth when he refused the rigor of a comprehensive education or later in his adulthood when he failed to undertake the mission of improving upon his character (assuming, of course, that he is in possession of his faculties). The fact that the average man finds it infinitely easier to remain in ignorance and stupidity does not bode well for the future of humanity as a whole. This kind of intellectual laziness alleviates a man from certain burdens that knowledge and understanding place upon him. Sympathy, instead, should be reserved for those who must attempt to deal earnestly with such a man.

65

The ethics of virtue is often criticized for not providing enough guidance with respect to what a man should do in any particular situation where he must make an ethical decision. Yet, no such principles exist or will ever exist that will convince a man entirely of their legitimacy. Law is the only recourse for those desiring specific moral direction, yet law is often infamously immoral and founded upon a slew of moral precepts which themselves lack foundation. Thus, it seems that no one can give a man specific moral guidance in such cases, only the *illusion* of guidance. After all, every situation is uniquely different — even its participants are never quite the same, though they may remain always experiencing their lives together. So a man presumes what he would do in what he imagines to be similar circumstances using varying degrees of rhetorical sophistication. Yet, a man can, at best, merely inspire a kind of direction to another man's life. He will not be able to force his views upon any man either by reason or by authority. Yet inspiration serves to awaken the man within, if he is receptive to it, toward perceiving his own inner depths and beginning the task of cultivating his character.

8

The State of Art

1

As the Greeks looked to Delphi for guidance and wisdom through poetic oracles that had to be interpreted by a high priest, the modern man should look to art and make of himself something of a holy cleric, skillfully interpreting meaning and understanding in the works of those great artistic souls who preceded him.

2

Man created God as a self-projection; a creation of a being who man most wished to emulate — a creation that man so desperately hoped to be someday. The entire project of history has been an effort to eclipse the fantasy and encounter the reality of this Being. Man wants to *be* God. It is the danger of which the Greeks warned man to avoid and the project with which he is nonetheless most concerned.

3

Whenever someone states that they believe the world would be unlivable without art, they are usually referring to their own — though they may include the work of others by extension, almost as if it were a blessing on their part. The absolute truth of the matter is that life is abundantly livable without art. What man finds impossible to live without is distraction. Although, to be sure, there are some distractions which are mistakenly referred to as art because they were painted on a canvas, written on a page, played with an instrument, or acted on the stage.

4

To the post-modern man and beyond: Your artists have failed you.

5

Mankind is at war, has been perpetually at war, perhaps will always be at war given his nature. It is a war for the survival of humanity against the tyranny of the inhumane. Sometimes this war is found to exist between countries, but this is merely its external manifestation. The first shot is always fired within the very heart of man himself. It is the responsibility of the artist to reveal the conflicts that exist within the human soul and forge a new perspective for mankind as a whole.

6

The artist, more than any other, if he is indeed worthy of the name, taps the spiritual realm and wrestles it into the existence of the everyday.

7

We have no need for any more warriors in our midst. The world is sickened with them. What we need is a warrior spirit in the artist who does battle with the ideas and feelings that cannot be otherwise expressed and defeats the forces of the abyss.

8

The human being, for all his powers, is limited and finite. He will never reach the pinnacle of ultimate understanding to his satisfaction nor be able to circumvent his destiny with death. He lives within a chaotic universe and attempts to create ways with which to deal with these facts by imagining an eternal heaven or a reasonable universe. The true meaning of life is to be found in the arts which promise, if they are truly beneficial arts, neither ultimate understanding nor comforting repose in some eternal resting place. These kinds of arts are themselves complex and irrational to a degree.

9

The mind of "God" is not to be understood by an examination of "His" creation but by *creating*.

10

The reason that artists create is the same reason that there are patrons of the arts. They all want to transcend the mundane experience of the human and participate in something seemingly divine, transformational, and ultimately soul-shaping. Art that has as its aim something other than these effects is merely distraction. It is the job of the artist to interpret the divine for each successive generation.

11

The depth found in any artist's work is often only the reflection of one's own depth. This is why the common man disdains the works of the greatest artists, not because he cannot comprehend them, but because he truly sees nothing there.

12

Life as it occurs is something rather unremarkable. It is only upon reflection that life gains its significance. Sometimes the moment itself allows for some reflection, but usually some time must pass and thought applied before one comes to realize the significance of anything in life. This is the function of art. An artist should be, above all else, a reflective man.

13

Making a living from one's art seems far more important to the artists of the late 20th and early 21st century than making art out of it.

14

A great deal of what man *feels* to be true is in error while much of what he has *rationally concluded* to be true is in error as well. While both may lead to error in the end, rationality, no doubt, corresponds better to the empirical perception of the world than does passion. Yet, when contemplating the higher truths, those which passion and reason are ill equipped to decipher on their own, man has created art.

15

High art possesses more complexity and subtlety than low art. Low art is similar to the hoots and grunts of another chimpanzee.

16

By its very nature society is a mindless and unconscious multitude of wills that seek to control the citizenry for its own greater good. Contemporary art, that pseudo-culture accepted by this tyrannical will, shall generally fail to last beyond the years in which it serves as a panacea or storm trooper for the society. Great art, on the other hand, that which lasts beyond a hundred years or so, is generally (though not always) the resistance of great men against this oppressive force of the unconscious will. Citizens that are not contemporaneous with a great work of art view it as a refreshing rebel who threatens them not at all.

17

All great art is moral by nature.

18

The only legacy worth leaving behind is one's thoughts for in them reside the soul of a man. His name is of little importance since it is nothing of his own doing and tells more about his parents than it does about himself. A man's deeds are likewise inconsequential since his deeds in relation to the universe around him seem petty and hardly worth mentioning. Life is fleeting and only holy to the man at rest, reflecting on life's magnificence and fragility. A man's accomplishments will eventually be recognized for what they are — the external shell of a man. To the man without much of a soul or an inner life, these are all he has to speak for him. Yet a man's thoughts, the inscribed monuments to his contemplation, even if they become misinterpreted (as they no doubt will be from time to time), still speak best for a man who is no longer able to speak for himself. A writer of stories or teller of tales, of course, leaves something behind of his inner life, but it is often distorted and leaves too much open for interpretation. The musician leaves behind the rhythm of his soul but man, again, must translate the product of this soul. Perhaps these artists are simply afraid to be judged too harshly and thus mask their souls in artifact.

19

The written word allows one into the thoughts of a man at his most honorable of hours. Thus one can be introduced to the possibilities inherent in mankind.

20

The higher man, one whose desire it is to fill his soul with wisdom, will not be able to do so without the presence of music in his life. For music speaks to the soul of a man like no other medium. Music is the language of the soul.

21

Even silence produces a kind of music, the rhythm of the abyss.

22

The wise have had to be witness to all of the great stupidities of man; watching as he wanders and stumbles along the way; watch as he battles his brothers for power, money, or pride; shake their heads as he attempts to become the master over all creation. This, however, was once the luxury of the wise. Now that man has acquired the means to destroy the world entire and all of the greatest achievements of mankind, the wise can no longer stand upon the mountaintop and look down upon these fools who may one day wipe away Shakespeare, Racine, Goethe, Emerson, Newton, and Schopenhauer from the cosmos. Instead, he must act and he must act in the only way that is available to him — in words and art.

23

Even the most successful and beloved of artists, who has composed the greatest of all masterpieces, is a sad, pathetic, and unenviable wretch whose life was merely sacrifice if he failed to compose his character in much the same way as he composed his masterpiece.

24

What is termed as genius is often little more than a fad.

25

The more an artist *attempts* to reach a larger demographic, the less he succeeds in creating a great work of art. This is not to say that art cannot be popular on occasion, but that art is not intended, nor does it usually attract, a mass audience. Once in awhile it might cause a stir among the mass public for one reason or another which causes the majority to arrive out of pure curiosity. They don't leave, however, having truly experienced anything transformative or soul-shaping — most simply shrug and walk away.

26

Of Shakespeare's tragic heroes, only Hamlet has any enduring value. The rest are utter fools. Perhaps this is why Shakespeare was known as the playwright of the people.

27

The work of art that attempts to appeal to the largest demographic of its time — that is, to sell itself as a mass commodity —will find itself passing away from existence around the same time, if not before, as the consumer who valued it.

28

Man's vanity with himself and his kind make him believe that there are no other worlds but his own in the universe. This same vanity allows him to likewise believe that he is in possession of the world's greatest art as well. Yet, the greatest man to have ever lived died in complete obscurity and his works, the most profound and awe inspiring ever created, were burned and buried with him by the tyrannical will of the inhumane.

29

The only art form that man truly cannot live for long without is music.

30

One can only escape death momentarily — immortality of the moment — through great art. This is not the experience of losing oneself in distraction, but the uniting that occurs between oneself and the greatest souls of antiquity — the collective soul of the ancients which reveals itself in the practice, study, and contemplation of art and philosophy. One transcends the earthly realm in a kind of shamanic unification with the ancestors for a brief period of time. It is a participation in the divine and the more one identifies himself with this realm of experience, the less daunting will seem his own individual demise.

31

Great art inspires the soul to wear a face and make its presence known.

32

The industrial age has brought forth a new breed of the mass man who fancies himself somehow superior to his less ambitious siblings. These are the pseudo-artists — those creatures who have found for themselves a niche amidst the world's huge stockpile of mediocrity by exploring their "creative" side. Some have a great deal of success peddling to the world's insatiable desire for distraction and amusement. Others prefer the languid squalor of the suffering bohemian — believing themselves somehow purer for the experience, wearing their despair as some sort of lifestyle. Yet, these souls are bereft of the burden that the artist endures — the urge to create something perfectly and exquisitely sublime, beautiful, divine; the urge to fashion a God from a simple strand of thread.

33

The reason to place artistic courage in higher regard than the courage of the warrior is that the latter cannot possibly fail. For the warrior, to fail is to die — an unfortunate event that brings with it two glories: 1) he will not then have to live with the defeat; and 2) his fellow men will still hold his sacrifice as sacred in their memory. The failure of artistic courage brings with it a necessity to live with the defeat, possibly for the remainder of one's life, and then listen to the snicker of one's fellows as they berate him for trying to reach the heights of human achievement.

34

The mass media has allowed the hack to employ himself as an artist. He lacks any semblance of insight, awareness, or profundity of perspective, but he does possess the talent of "spectacle" and this should be the moniker of the entire age.

35

Great art rebels against both the left and the right hands for it is centered in the heart of man.

36

Art cannot compete with entertainment in the same manner that love cannot compete with sex.

37

One should be somewhat wary of the modern bohemian. They will spend hours in each others company, speaking eloquently about their painting, writing, or song. Yet, a true artist only fits in his art. Thus, he would have little motivation to congregate in the first place and far too little time to spend conversing in the second.

38

To choose art as a profession is to oftentimes not choose art at all.

39

The art of the industrial age is more inclined to hold a mirror up to society rather than nature. More often than not, it then ceases to be art and transforms into propaganda.

40

Modern man has tried to invent new forms in order to give relevance to that which never went out of style. He should instead pay more attention to substance.

41

It has become the endeavor of the artist to legitimize himself by profession rather than by his work. This is quite understandable since creating a career is much easier than creating a work of art and society puts a greater premium upon one's profession than it does upon one's worth. The true artist, however, must see through this illusion and focus his attention on those elements of his work that are important.

42

The art of the industrial age is not merely reflecting the consciousness of its time. Rather, it has become poisoned by it.

43

I can often hear the cry in the souls of men to the artists of the modern age: "Speak to me about the conditions of our time so that I might better understand them." Such a cry is then followed by an empty sigh that the resulting art did little to satisfy. The cry, however, should be amended for the artists to speak of everything immemorial. The rest is superfluous.

44

One should not attempt to live the life of an artist, but instead internalize an artistic perspective. The lives of artists themselves are typically far too impulsive, bohemian, and flighty to serve as an inspiring model. In fact, a good many are despicable characters indeed. How they perceived the world is the crucial factor for the higher man, not how they engaged in it.

45

Anything that can be rightly considered "cultural" must first be cultivated — some raw passion nurtured and refined into something beautiful or sublime.

46

The artist perceives the world with the eyes of a dying man.

47

The great artist will rarely ever see the fruits of his labor validated externally as such work must germinate and ferment within the soil of the majority for quite some time before it may ever come to seed. Therefore, he will need a special kind of inner faith in himself that his labors are worth their effort. This should not be too difficult for the true artist, however, since he understands his work as providing him with meaning and significance.

48

The true artist will sojourn on in his work even if he has neither admirers nor any compensation for his efforts. It is, after all, a labor of passion. A woman does not abandon her child simply because the tyke is not pleasing to the rest of the world. A pseudo-artist, of course, will dispense with his projects as soon as he discerns that the work will not suit as a career. He wishes to *be* an artist while the true artist simply *is* one.

49

Science explains, or at least hopes to explain, the nature of how things are constituted and how they might have come to be. It only asks "why" in relation to this overall concern for "how." The artistic preoccupation is primarily an attempt to answer the question of "why."

50

A man understands his life and the profundity of his existence better through art than through theory because this is how he actually experiences it — as an observer and interpreter. He is not so much a pure intellect as he is a feeler, thinker, and intuitor.

51

Art is that which resonates with a more profound and deep significance, providing life with the kind of meaning which it does not inherently possess. How often a simple piece of music seems to make all of creation suddenly spring to life or a poem provides just the right insight into what was otherwise concealed.

52

For the most part, art of popular culture exists to stupefy the masses and assuage the petty grievances of their quivering hearts. If it informs a man's life, it does so pedantically and then only with those lessons approved by the status quo. Such art is merely a trinket of distraction designed to mollify a man's unpleasant connection to the world.

53

A man indulges in distraction as a means of escaping the cold reality of his existence. A man immerses himself in art, however, in order to directly confront the harsh realities of his life and find meaning and deeper significance to that which seems at times devoid of both.

54

True art exposes the pettiness of everyday life as something superficial and unworthy of man's attention, revealing the depth and profundity of those sublime elements of existence, but for which mankind would have no reason to continue forward.

55

Great art addresses a different kind of truth than great science. It is the truth of the imagination, the spirit — that great "nothingness" that is not reducible to the particles of matter. There is no room for God in science and this is as it should be, for reason should have no master but itself when determining the physical nature of the universe. Yet, there is ample space for God in art and far too few men willing to view their religion as such. So, they cling to the tenets of their book as a miser does to gold, both seeking refuge from their own cowardice.

56

Heidegger recognized that one of the worst consequences of technology is to perceive the human as little more than a resource, a means to some greater end, thus relegating humanity to the status of a mere commodity. This "commodification" of the human makes of his art a commercial endeavor as well, the value of which is placed upon its marketability. Thus the artist is forced to judge his work on its commercial viability rather than its aesthetic composition or the depths of its perception. In fact, he will only be even considered an artist when he puts his work up for sale and it is subsequently purchased. The aim of the work then is preconceived in favor of diversion and entertainment rather than as a transmitter of that which is most divine in man.

57

The artist is the conscience of any society as well as its estimator of value.

58

The idea of "God" is an artistic creation. It makes the divine something concrete and understandable so that life can be perceived as something greater than its mere appearance might show.

59

The true artist has always served the function of a certain kind of prophet — if not expressing the exact perspective or mind of "God," then at least concerned with that which is divine in some sense. The false prophet, meanwhile, is the modern day entertainer.

60

Science speaks the language of the concrete and the verifiable while poetry and art are the voice of the abstract and the spiritual. To expect science to provide a deeper understanding of the meaning of life or the spirit would be akin to composing a symphony in order to drive a nail.

61

Philosophers are nothing more nor less than artists creating in the medium of reason.

62

Naïve art is that which depicts a world that has been created primarily as a product of wish fulfillment. Fundamental to this kind of work is the false depiction of reality that it *must* display in order to create such a thing.

63

The difficulty of creating art is that the artist is often not internally strong enough to be possessed by his artistic vision and it consequently ruins his life.

64

Man has, throughout the centuries, sought to find the unifying principle of existence, human nature, or morality in the vain hope that such a theory might provide him with a certain peace of mind, absolving him of his suffering. Yet, no authentic man actually lives his life according to the directives of a theory, no matter how useful, comprehensive or cohesive it may prove to be. Theory itself should be simply admired as something of a work of art, the construct of an intelligent mind engaged in the attempt to form dissonant noise into music.

65

Both philosophy and art (and here I would include the masterpieces of religion as well) are merely suggestive of truth and the good life. The higher purpose of man, assuming that he is willing and able to suspend his pathological need for contentment, is to passionately immerse himself, almost single-mindedly, in the exploration of these works (as many as he has time to examine) and painstakingly build the edifice of his soul from those pieces that most honestly appeal to his better nature, some he will find he shares in common with his fellow men and he will call these "universal truths" and others will speak to him alone. Regardless, it is his duty, if he desires a greatness of spirit, to construct his life from the ideas found in the rubble of the dreams of other great souls.

9

The State of Reflection and the Individual

1

The introvert is thought to somehow suffer from a lack of experience with the world, as if a man who withdraws inward cannot possibly gain all of the wonderful advantages available to the extrovert whose inclusion of a wide diversity of people and conversation into his habitat is thought to be a vastly superior means to attaining a rich and extensive sense of self. Yet, while it is true that the extrovert gathers more experience around him, it is merely of a quantitative nature and often is substantively weaker in quality than the experience of the introvert. The extrovert, for instance, may discuss any number of topics in an hour with his fellows, but between them, they may only utter a single thing of any real value. The rest of their time is spent in small talk, mindless banter, and the hoots of camaraderie shared by men who are barely acquainted with one another. In solitude, however, a man will not allow himself to talk to his soul in such a manner.

2

Only in solitude will a man consort with himself. The less time he spends in that condition, the more he will bend to the will of others — so lacking will he be in a soul of his own.

3

To fear solitude is to fear oneself.

4

Man's a social animal as much as he is animal, but solitary if he should wish to rise above the beast.

5

If a man does not separate himself from the cacophony of the world, he will never hear his own voice distinctly.

6

Everywhere man is caught in the whir of distraction that will not allow him a moment's contemplation. So much so that he eventually considers these distractions to be the fundamental activity of his life. However, it is the reverse that is true. A man immersed for hours in contemplation is he who is closest to his nature.

7

People cultivate friendships as a distraction.

8

It is not, as Aristotle suggests, the "nature" of man to live with others. It is his condition. From the moment of his birth even prehistoric man awoke to find himself suckled to his family.

9

Idleness is only a sin if it lacks in contemplation.

10

Those spirits that are not suited for contemplation, and there are multitudes, have no real need for leisure.

11

Few understand solitude because they cannot conceive of self construction as a kind of achievement, let alone the most important accomplishment of all. Solitude, to them, is merely an idle wasting of one's time. Since it does nothing to procure material gain, it is assumed to be the occupation of the languid and sluggish ne'er-do-well.

12

A man cannot, to be sure, spend the entirety of his life in contemplative solitude. Without engagement with the rest of the world, whether past or present, there would exist very little to contemplate.

13

Socializing, unless one travels in very rarified circles, does little more than kill time and, by extension, oneself.

14

Is man a social creature, or is he not first (the womb) and last (death) a creature of isolation?

15

It would seem that whenever people gather together their perception dulls significantly.

16

Boredom comes easily to he who hasn't much in his life to contemplate.

17

No man should exist *for* others, yet he most certainly must exist *with* others. Therefore, if he is to be wise, he must learn when it is appropriate to compromise and when he must stand firm in his resolve. Human history is replete with infamous examples of men who were either entirely ignorant of this distinction or not at all astute at recognizing the proper path in context to the situation in which he found himself.

18

The great man must have the courage to set out alone on his quest for understanding since his contemporaries shall be of little help to him. He will be like a man in exile from his time, though he will have the wisdom of the ages to accompany him. Yet, these books merely serve as a foundation upon which to set his feet and begin the task at hand.

19

The higher purpose for words or language is to inspire. Any book should lead you to thoughts of your own, otherwise put it down. The same is true of acquaintances.

20

The role of the prophet is to speak truth to power and there exists no better exemplar of this principal than that moment when the rebellious angels confronted God. And what was the pronouncement that warranted their expulsion? For what truth were they so willing to refuse the request of a divine? The notion that, overall, man is not worthy of their respect.

21

A man needs his fellow man in order to survive, but they are often a hindrance in his attempts to live.

22

A man's family is not the one that he is born into, but the one that he has freely chosen.

23

If a man should wish fortune upon you, look upon it not with ease, for he is filled with wishes and thoughts more abundant and severe than these within him.

24

The majority of men live unsatisfactory lives primarily out of cowardice and conformity.

25

Consider all the attempts made to bring one into the norm. The entire aim of education is a covert design for socialization. Yet, this process of normalization is not presided over by some evil genius with plans for world domination. Man created it from his own neurosis, his own desire to blend into the immortal crowd. Hitler did not rise to power on his own. Man created him. He let the monster reign. Why? Because he is so afraid to stand alone.

26

There are those (and they are many) who believe it somehow to be a punishment to die alone. They wish for it upon their enemies. They fear it for themselves. It's as if death itself was not terrible enough, but to die alone somehow makes it all the more horrific. Death, they can abide. Solitude must be assuaged with companions whenever possible. Most men on their deathbed, if they are so blessed with an opportunity for a few final moments of reflection, will reach instead to pull their family closer to them. They fail to realize that everyone shall die alone. The comfort they receive is merely an illusion.

27

Given the choice between honest reflection and mindless entertainment, the modern will invariably choose the latter.

28

Man must be anesthetized to live in such a modern world, even one of his own design. For try as he might, he is still human after all.

29

The pale rebel will not rebel among his companions for fear that they will exclude him. The true radical and revolutionary spirit is profoundly alone.

30

To be the imitator of many, perhaps that is the structure of the true individual. He is a synthesis of a multiplicity of perspectives into a whole new and unique personality.

31

Only in death does one "become" anything. Even those poor souls who lazily refuse to expend the necessary energy to develop the upward growth of the soul still become and change. Their maturation though, if one can call it such, resembles something of a knotty, twisted, and broken oak.

32

The masses declare that the authentic life is the one lived not according to a man's own cultivated desires or even necessarily to his advantages but with the advancement of all humanity in mind. In this manner his principles and actions should be geared toward what his talents might allow to move humanity forward and transcend the innate "animalism" of his existence. However, such a perspective is of the authentic "society" man, the follower and the interchangeable man to a certain degree. It is, of course, true that the vast majority of men, when left to seek their own desires and advantages, will almost necessarily be lead by their lesser natures into an assortment of vices that benefit neither themselves nor others. Thus arises society's compulsion for controlling such characters. Yet, it does not make a man less authentic for pursuing these desires; it merely makes him less significant to the mob.

33

Authenticity is an abstraction like justice, love, or freedom; each is a complex idea that is slightly different for everyone and is often defined by what it is not.

34

One must be, essentially, selfish to the very core — though not in the childish sense that Rand suggests. The discovery of one's soul, at first, requires a concern and perhaps even an obsession with the self to the exclusion of all others. However, this is merely its origin, its youth. Eventually it extends out to others as well, as it must. Yet, if the core of a man's being is not uniquely his own, he cannot possess anything of possible value to give to others. Nothing of any true value anyway.

35

The creation of one's self, its construction into a thing of beauty, is the only task of a great soul.

36

To possess the courage to stand alone, ironically, places one in the company of all the other great souls who came before. This is small recompense to those weaker natures who would rather be wrong and stand shoulder to shoulder with living fools.

37

Oftentimes a man who considers himself a rebel will only be moved to revolution if he is accompanied by the crowd.

38

The problem with America is that its citizens are primarily herd animals who are of the mistaken belief that somehow they are instead fierce individualists. In fact, they all clamor in unison so that they might bleat out their pathetic song while ignoring the voices of the 100,000 other sheep who are warbling the same ridiculous tune.

39

Even the individual must know his proper place within the larger structure of a society if he is to realize himself.

40

The man with few equals will only be crowned as such, if at all, after he has died.

41

Until one comes face to face with the ultimate meaninglessness and sheer emptiness of his life, despite the accoutrements that he has attached to himself to help negate this terrible realization, he will never truly succeed in knowing himself. Only then can he begin to connect with his true self and respond honestly to his world — a world which has no need of him whatsoever. Ironically, when he does finally achieve this realization, he can also begin to fashion a meaning and uniqueness to his existence that can provide significance to the rest of the world.

42

There are others, alas, the vast majority of men, who will catch a glimpse of this nothingness of existence and cower before it instead of undertaking the challenge of forging ahead to make a meaningful life and creating value from nothing. Committing what Camus referred to as "philosophical suicide," they will deny what they've seen, settling in to some established, traditional mode of meaning and spend their days distracting themselves from what they perceive as their unfortunate encounter with the abyss.

43

The best defense against tyranny — essentially the only defense — is individuation. Those who would gather forces and arm themselves against tyranny create, in a sense, another tyranny.

44

At every turn, one is faced with the prospect of conformity. It seems the entire world is concerned with every individual becoming less of one, as if that were the project of humanity. The fight against this force might seem daunting at times, even perhaps a pessimistic endeavor, but must ultimately be won if a man is to successfully lift himself from out of the doldrums that seek his ruin.

45

The nonconformist is truly a conformist if he chooses nonconformity for its own sake. Instead, the true rebel must decide at times to follow the crowd when it suits his nature to do so.

46

Nietzsche would have us say "Yes" to life — to every petty injustice or barbaric atrocity of man. He would then wish for us to adore these fates to such an extent that we would live them out eternally. However, as Nietzsche did himself with his work, one must say "No" to any variety of stupidities and apocalyptic nightmares that occur because man inflicts his twisted will upon the world. Only by saying "no" to those things which a man must rebel against can he help to shape a destiny that he might wish to perpetuate eternally. Otherwise, he is merely a helpless leaf blown by whatever breeze happens to flutter by. It is not a goal of perfection that he seeks but the goal of achieving something acceptable to his own individual nature.

47

As soon as a man declares himself a Christian, a Buddhist, a Taoist, an artist or the like, he is already lost, for he will have fashioned himself upon some preconceived notion of each. He should instead be able to declare that he is all of these and more at once.

48

It would seem as if the world would have man's focus be perpetually away from his own person, as if individuality were a dreaded disease from which the world must rid itself. To this end, the world's religions congregate. Yet, the greatest achievements of humanity are often produced by the man who works alone.

49

Beware all men who wish to include you in their communion. Though they may claim to have your interests in mind, they are secretly building a quorum.

50

Love will sometimes attempt to conquer one's own self regard — often when one needs it most.

51

The cult of individuality will soon collapse to enable the true individuals to arise alone.

52

You are what you read, regurgitating your "wisdom" to the world.

53

No society can stand to have too many unique and individual souls for citizens. It needs a few, no doubt, to keep it from stagnating and this is the role of the artist and thinker. However, the utopian ideal of a society of uniquely exceptional spirits will break down soon enough when each individual refuses to compromise for the greater good. At best, a society can tolerate pseudo-individuals who believe themselves unique and self-reliant when, in fact, they are simply deluded by self love.

54

Even the mob has its rightful place among the rank of men.

55

Singular man cannot escape collective man entirely, yet he must be vigilant that he not be consumed by it.

56

"I" is merely the sum total of consciousness at any particular point in time.

57

Nonconformity is the only valid human response to a world gone mad. Yet a man must be vigilant to remain a nonconformist among the nonconformists as well. And, of course, remember to maintain his humor.

58

There are too many fools who dress themselves in bizarre fashions and whose lifestyle or behaviors demonstrate a kind of intentional peculiarity which they then mistake for nonconformity. Yet, such fools lack a conviction for which they might take a stand. Instead, they stand against something else, often anything else, because they identify with the rebel even if they don't have his higher aim. In essence, they wish to join the rebellion without having much concern for the cause — they simply wish to fit in somewhere.

59

There is an obvious immaturity to being a nonconformist for the mere sake of nonconformity. The trick is to develop and cultivate one's own inner nature — to nurture it and let it flourish. Only then will you discover your own uniqueness — one that will only conform to those ideas and perspectives that arise from within and be repelled by those which are foreign to you.

60

The religion of nonconformity proposes too many dogmas and, ironically, produces a congregation of lemmings.

61

When you instruct a man to be a nonconformist, in a sense you are asking that he conform.

62

The vast majority who egotistically believe themselves to be unique individuals are truly little more than mindless drones — little bees buzzing about.

63

To believe one's own thought to be distinctively one's own is ignorance. To ignore one's own thought because it is not original is suicide.

64

Mill writes that "eccentricity has always abounded when and where strength of character has abounded." Apparently he did not foresee eccentricity practiced as a kind of fad wherein it demonstrates a neuroticism, an insecurity, and a decided *weakness* of character.

65

A man who grants favor to the opinion of the mob often gives little credence to his own.

66

It is generally assumed that the radical must first be political. Of course, the vast majority of radicals are political in nature, but what animates their collective action is the radical of a different kind — the essential radical. He is the man who views *life* from a different perspective rather than simply through the lens of politics, laws, and rights and in so doing may just tweak the vision of all humanity. The very last of those to acknowledge and finally adopt his new dynamic picture of the universe are politicians who then codify it into law.

67

Beware of those who would wish to have you live your life within some ready made theoretical delusion. The philosopher, for example, who would like you to believe that all the world is animated by some kind of will. Humanity, however, is not an equation and can never neatly fit within the doctrines meant to confine it.

68

You must be prepared to fall astray of even the rebels of your day if you truly wish to be a rebel.

69

Individualism at the expense of another is simply greed — as foul a commodity as a king who feasts before the starving beggars.

70

Passivity can sometimes be a form of rebellion.

71

One must do his best to avoid all patriots and zealots in his daily life. He should also feel significantly uneasy if he finds himself in agreement with them in argument as well. The patriot and the zealot are products of the mob and as such they have no brain. A man should refrain from their company lest his individuality become enveloped in their wave of madness.

72

Man honors and celebrates those people who act in a manner that justifies his own ideals. Yet, those heroes have done him no favors and merely serve to possibly further strengthen his own illusions. He would be better served to turn his attention to those exceptional spirits who do not represent the creeds of the greater mass of men. Only then might he expect to learn something worthwhile.

73

Better to be afflicted with one's own insanity than that of another.

74

It is more noble, more praiseworthy, to fail in the peerless pursuit than to succeed, at the highest level, in the unworthy one championed by the multitudes.

75

The true individual makes no attempt to compete with others. He hasn't the need, for he knows that he's already won in the simple act of competing solely with himself. This is one of the most difficult endeavors of the individual.

76

Only man gives much consideration to the individual in nature because he himself desperately wishes to be distinct and unique to the world. Yet, he is, in the majority, ill equipped to undertake the necessary sacrifice in order to make himself distinctive. He is far more comfortable moving within the undifferentiated collective, doing what is expected of him and thinking little for himself. Individuality, it is true, is a specifically human value, but most humans only admire it from afar, fearing that it will eventually bring them ruin, unwilling to undergo the considerable challenges of cultivating one's character to bring it to fruition.

77

A man becomes alienated as soon as he begins to set himself apart as an individual. It is merely his lot in life if he wishes to be something more than just a cog in the great machine.

78

Do not confuse individuality with stubborn childishness. The true individual is most engaged in battling *against* his own egotistical wishes and desires precisely because they seek to control him. In this manner, the ego impedes the progress of an individual. To live by the precepts of the soul and not the rules of society or your own egotistical desires, *that* is individuality.

79

The individual attempts to transcend himself in order to participate in some greater overall experience. More often than not, he will attempt to do so by uniting himself with the human collective. He will surrender his individuality to the rest of humanity because he views their cause as something greater than himself. The collective, however, is only greater than those individuals whose character is lacking some essential virtue. The true individual is always something greater than the whole bleating stable of mankind put together. He will find his transcendence only through individual experience with the sublime.

80

The greatest thing about man, that which continues to give him resolve, is that he is able to transcend the conditions of his birth as a collective being and rise to the heights of a unique and singular individual. This event, however, does not happen naturally.

81

The great delusion of the herd, that which they devise to soothe their wounded conscience and make it possible for them to justify their pathetic existence, is the shared belief that they are, in fact, wolves instead of cattle.

82

In science, any valid theory admits to its being only the temporary manifestation of truth, but this is its strength and the reason why science will always win out over religion — it does not arrogantly suppose itself to be in possession of the ultimate knowledge of existence. Its awareness of the truth is of a more humble variety. It passionately gathers all of the available evidence and posits a model that suits all relevant facts, prepared, all the while, to abandon the notion when either new information is obtained or a better theory arises. The theory, in other words, is not sacred, only the method can be considered something worthy of devotion. This should be the model used by the individual as well as he constructs the entity of his character.

83

There are no accidents, not because of the will of some divine consciousness, but because of your own, conscious and unconscious, choices. There are, then, no excuses as well.

84

One does not choose one's character in any significant sense. After all, so much is already given to a man at birth. Rather, a man discovers his character and molds it to its best expression given his circumstances and the contents of his being. This is one of the projects to which he must commit himself — the discovery of the better nature of his own unique character. Yet, the problem that arises is how one should come to know which elements of himself are superior to others. It cannot, of course, simply be those qualities which are to one's liking since, intuitively, the contented murderer does not seem to be an admirable character. They also don't appear to be qualities commendable by a simple majority, susceptible as men are to the mediocrity of the norm. Yet, superior qualities are a factor of consensus to a certain degree. They are traits that have stood the test of time as being something valued by the great men of the past. These are virtues such as kindness, loyalty, humor, courage, moderation, justice, generosity, humility, tolerance, and compassion. This list is only partial, of course, and not every virtue will suit the particular character of every man, yet the sentiments of other great souls serve as a kind of guide to help a man along the way in discovering the best features of his own true and genuine personality.

85

The criminal, of course, is a unique individual to the extent that he rebels against the norms of his society; however, he lacks the necessary wisdom as to which traits constitute the cultivation of his *higher* nature.

86

Selfishness is not a virtue unless it is applied exclusively to the development of one's own soul. To this end, a great man must totally disregard what he owes to his fellow men.

87

Men too often rely on the assessment of others to determine the reality of their nature, as if to be an artist required a contingency of other people to agree that it were so, even though the assessment of others is often wrong. Instead, one needs a certain amount of faith in one's own judgment regardless of the external facts. Though, too, he must remain stringently honest with his critique of himself. A man unable to trust his own honest assessment is a lonely man indeed.

88

The temptation to delude oneself is sometimes too provocative to bear alone so a man calls for his friends to join him.

89

A man must be willing to tell himself the most hurtful of truths, the most devastating of conclusions, in order to ensure that he does not become a victim of his own delusions. Yet, he must be willing to recognize his better qualities as well and not mistake them for traits that he would rather do without. In short, a man must develop a certain wisdom and honesty about himself.

90

All modern men are in a significant sense alienated from the world in which they live and the people who live in it. Yet, whereas the common man fervently strives to alleviate this condition, the great man derives from it a certain power and seeks to further sequester himself from the world in order to discover what additional fruits it might yield.

91

In order to be truly genuine in his character a man must first realize where his place is within the external world — where does he fit? After all, a man is more than just his inner nature. He is a fool who desires to be an actor but is not at home upon the stage or in the theatre and forces himself upon that world. Instead, he must find a place where he belongs, a place that is suited to his talents and the better aspects of his nature.

92

Personal desires and feelings should be, to a certain extent, viewed as childish impulses. They cannot be given too much credibility in determining what a man should do. They differ from intuition in the sense that they are wedded to the ego of a man, so much so that they inhibit his perspective of himself and his world and lead him primarily into suffering. They are in need of significant cultivation to be utilized effectively.

93

One's outer self is only false when it fails to coexist harmoniously with the better part of one's inner nature. The problem is, of course, that man is constantly mistaken about what constitutes his best attributes. Usually he errs on the side of following his uncultivated passions.

94

Authenticity is hardly the desired goal of a life well lived for any individual. After all, a man can be an authentic ass.

95

As important as it is to judge one's own character honestly, it is equally important to acquire the skill of honestly judging the character of others as well.

96

The individual rebel alone will attain freedom for himself and may inspire others to do the same while the revolutionary, in freedom's name, will merely lead men into another form of bondage.

97

"I am special! I am unique! There is not another like me in all the world!" So sayeth the shepherd. So sayeth the flock. Yet, methinks the fools doth protest too much.

98

Men constantly struggle against the restraints of fate and circumstance, contending to demonstrate to fortune that it is they who control their own destiny. Yet, rarely do they attempt to free their mind from this need to exercise dominion which is the drive of the ego for power over all.

99

Social cohesion, the kind which desires peaceful, untroubled, and unexamined coexistence, is always endangered by the eccentrics, the contrarians, the rebels, and the mad. Yet, it is just such characters who often provide a necessary and valuable perspective for such a cloistered and incestuous society.

100

The staunch individualist, who believes that in living alone he is abandoning his reliance on others, can only fancy such a notion at a time absent of any crisis.

101

The shrill individualist, he who often esteems himself above all rightful measure and rails against all forms of collectivism, conveniently forgets that any kind of social organization is a collective of one sort or another, without which he would have perished long ago — his prideful and egotistical existence devoured by the indifference of nature.

102

The modern man commonly searches the work of science, philosophy, and art, if he peruses them at all, in order to find justifications for his most cherished personal beliefs rather than as inspirations that might alter his perspective.

103

A man is only truly free in so much as he allows his mind to be — the rest will find him a slave in one fashion or another.

104

Tyranny is, and always has been, an establishment of the people. No one king or leader has ever reigned tyrannical without consent, tacit or otherwise. In fact, there can be no such thing as a society without some form of tyranny for its rule. The ideas and concerns of a nation of people are agreed upon by the majority, whether by silent accord or with determined intent. Yet, the majority of men are short-sighted, egotistical, ambitious, fearful, deluded, and unwise. In America, where they pride themselves on their individuality and freedom from oppression, they have cultivated the tyranny of the "average man;" the widespread cultural malaise of conformity to fashion. They worship at the altar of mediocrity and admonish those as "elitist" who would suggest that excellence should be the standard judgment of a man; excellence not simply in one small portion of a man's life, but in its totality. However, such a proposal is anathema to most Americans who neither wish to be thought inadequate nor desire to invest the resources necessary to be otherwise. Instead, they rejoice in their conformity and celebrate in their conceit of unique individuation. They pander to the ideas and the interests of an unworthy majority. Thus, America has become, despite her formidable youth, the quintessential land of insignificance. She cherishes petty things and exalts the trivial to an art. The "average" man has become the ideal and he, in turn, strives to possess all things ordinary — money, land, power, and inner peace

105

The fool who believes there would be little lost to humanity if a few imbeciles were subtracted, does not conceive of the possibility that he is one of them.

10

The State of Society

1

Plato, it seems, did not foresee the flaws of his Republic. While he conceived of the most perfect political formation the world has ever known in theory, it is utterly untenable in practice for a variety of reasons, notably: philosopher kings are few and far between, sometimes only appearing every century or so. While Plato's philosophical university may gain its students knowledge, it is at a loss to grant them wisdom, the most important component for such a king. Contrary to popular belief, wisdom does not merely come with age and education.

2

Society is the attempt to bring all of its citizens to a shared understanding of normalcy. Even the long held deification of individualism is nothing more than a society's restriction on the individual. It propagates this idea in its citizens in order for them to conclude that their potential success or failure within the system is one that is within their own control. In other words, it provides the illusion of hope wherein despondency would be a more proper response. Yet, society would desire to wish away despondency since it is unproductive. It serves no societal need and does nothing more than deepen the human character. Yet, it is precisely this deepening of character that is necessary for the men with a certain "greatness of soul" to emerge.

3

Distrust all beliefs that you hold in common with the majority of men. You will, of course, hold certain sentiments in common with your contemporaries, otherwise morality would be impossible, but beliefs are bred of experience and wisdom and, as such, they should be uniquely your own.

4

The society that allows for the "voice of the people" to dictate policy will eventually learn that the "people" are profoundly unqualified for such a responsibility. The mass of men find it too difficult to look beyond their own myopic concerns and society soon suffers from a kind of slavish mediocrity and eventual decay. A great man may come along every so often to lead them to a place of prominence, but more often than not they are lead by a charlatan piper whose tune merely sirens the masses to the wasteland of human folly. Similarly, the society that relinquishes power to a select few will inevitably find that philosopher kings arrive upon the scene less frequently than previously believed and that tyrants are far more prevalent.

5

Society finds it much easier to judge a man's value based upon his assets and his net worth. A man's assets are simply those tangible possessions that can be exchanged for monetary value. His net worth is nothing more than the total sum of his assets. Thus, it is easy to judge the worth of a man by merely calculating the financial gains that he might claim as his own. Worth is thus determined by a rather simple mathematical equation. While the artists all attempt to demonstrate otherwise, and though the masses will compute the sum total of a man's friends into the calculation as well, it is nonetheless true that the world predominately values those qualities which lack complexity.

6

Mankind so despises complexity because it is a constant reminder of his place in the universe. Thus, he forever attempts to simplify the world and bring it down to his size.

7

The notions of justice and law are incorporated into the human drama not as a means to some divine truth, but as an attempt to create a God in a world in which there isn't one.

8

The warrior is merely the protector and enforcer of the state. As Thoreau observes, such a man serves as like a body to the head. Yet, never will you see in one individual someone who is extraordinarily strong in body as well as in mind since the development of each requires considerable sacrifice that will necessarily preclude the other. The warrior is little more than a brute who, if he ever begins to set his puny mind to think, will need to be controlled.

9

Men have often made the mistake of ordering their societies in a vain attempt to order their own hearts. I imagine this occurs because it's easier to tame and pacify others than the rebellious nature of one's own soul.

10

There exists the world as you experience it and the world as you might wish for it to be. Society is man's attempt to reconcile these two worlds and make them appear somewhat similar in nature.

11

Cultivation and domestication are two completely distinctive things. The latter subdues while the former improves.

12

Man has allowed himself to become little more than a social creature — a player upon an enormous stage, forgetting all the while that he's playing a character. A character that may be, in some small part, connected to himself; however, he soon mistakes the part for the whole and the totality of himself, his authentic being, is lost in the process.

13

The difficulty of intuition, for the state, is that it cannot be as easily controlled as reason or the passions. It has a "mind" of its own which owes its loyalty to life in general and the individual in particular.

14

Human progress has been abandoned for technological progress to such an extent that man now imagines the progress of the human to *be* technological. The actual progress of the human meanwhile meanders and falls into places which only serve to regress it. Human progress seems to be biding its time much as an adolescent awaits adulthood, but without the promise that it will arrive.

15

All men are not endowed by their creator with certain inalienable rights any more than their creator bore them to be equal to one another. This idea is a creation of mankind itself and shows the power inherent in the human imagination. Yet, just as man creates, he also destroys.

16

The inalienable rights bestowed on man should be conferred on many other animals as well but for man's seemingly limitless overestimation of his own worth.

17

Society will generally discourage the experiencing of ecstasies which do not serve the purposes of the state. In fact, the state will whole-heartedly go to war against them as these ecstasies threaten the very existence of the state. The state generally endorses stupefying drugs or states of being (unless these factors inhibit production) because such conditions serve the needs of the society in that stupefied citizens are easier to govern. Individuals who partake in ecstasies that allow a heightened or altered perception of reality that is different than the state-sponsored perception will gradually come to the realization that reality or truth is multivariate and an essentially perspectival phenomenon that is overwhelmingly complex and nothing more than the creation of the human mind. This realization, of course, will lead one to call into question all manner of rules, laws, and governing philosophies since the only truth for him will be that there is no truth outside of the perception of man. Yet, the truth of man, derived from the mind of man and with certain aspects shared in common with other men, can still lead to a conclusion of meaning, order, and law even if that meaning has no other foundation than his own mind — lie to him though it does at times. To deny man then his ecstasies or his altered perceptions is to deny him the truth about himself. Of course, there are men who indulge in ecstasies as a means of *escaping* the true nature of their existence rather than as an attempt to connect with it. As with all things, the character of a man and his intentions will determine his connection to what is worthy and true. Unfortunately, the vast majority of men are not imbued with much in the way of character. They indulge in ecstasies in much the same manner that a suicide amuses himself with Russian roulette.

18

In the present age it seems that men are constantly engaged in reasoning when they should be trusting in the verities of their soul and faithfully following their passions when they should be letting reason have the say. In other words, present man is almost entirely backward about everything.

19

Sanity, to the madman, often appears as a form of madness.

20

The capitalist mantra that "the customer is always right" is nothing short of a beggar's belief. The man who proclaims such an idea is betraying his own inferiority, even in the face of someone who may be otherwise inferior to him — especially so in such a case.

21

Wealth and privilege never made a man a whit more wise. The elites of possession and opportunity are usually quite common in character, if not altogether bereft of it.

22

Educating the masses, while perhaps a noble intent, is ultimately a fruitless pursuit beyond a certain point. True education, whose aim is directed beyond the machinery of state necessity, is reserved for the elite alone. Only they can appreciate it and be trusted to use it for something more than their own material propagation. Education is not a tool, but a way of understanding — a continuous development, sophistication, and deepening of the human character that must first be recognized as something desirable to a man.

23

An appeal to tradition is a confession that the speaker has given little thought as to why he believes as he does. The belief has simply been his custom and the tacitly agreed upon habits of his compatriots (all of whom having decided the matter in a similar fashion).

24

Society bestows moral value upon actions that seem to be lacking in ego — selflessness, compassion, self-denial — because these best serve the state and not the individual. They help the state to flourish and thereby provide for the majority. The egotistic act is admonished as something lower, though it be the true motive for any human action. Thus, do all men feel guilty when they recognize it within themselves. So, the artificial actions are determined to be the "moral" ones and the natural actions are less worthy of consideration. Yet, "good" or "bad" with respect to actions is merely a wise or foolish distinction serving to balance individual flourishing with communal flourishing. It is not a morally commendable or "good" person who helps out his fellow man. The man instead is wise because the act benefits him by providing a feeling of self-worth and a sense of belonging to a community within which he is supported while at the same time providing the community with the support of its citizens, without which it could not survive in the first place. No moral act was committed whereby we can then dub the individual as "good," but we can certainly determine him to be wise on occasion.

25

Prison is not the place for those who are morally bankrupt (there are, after all, plenty of reprobates who remain free). It is the place for those who do not, for whatever reason, abide by the contractual obligations of society. Prison is only rehabilitative as far as it is successful in its attempt to change the offender's perspective with respect to his attitude toward the law and such a change in perception will never be effectively coerced for long.

26

Just because a man is allowed by his society to express and hold any opinion whatsoever does not mean that opinions should not be subject to ridicule and derision. Of course, the problem is that opinions which cut across the grain of the majority are often ridiculed, not because they are untrue, but because they are unpopular. After all, Einstein on an island of morons would be regarded as the dolt of his community.

27

Great spirits view the state similar to the manner that an adult views the rules of his parents — with amusement.

28

Most cultures celebrate diversity as long as that diversity does not include foundationally different beliefs and ideas.

29

Political leaders are never culled from the herd of great men. Rather they are chosen for their capacity to project the greatest attributes of the mob. The mob, in this sense, constructs its own ideal prototype.

30

From the child's perspective, a mature adult is one who acts appropriately and behaves according to the norms of mature society. In other words, the adult is one who is dressed in the garbs of external maturity. He behaves as he's supposed to behave and looks as he's supposed to look, according to the beliefs and fashions of the day. How does one expect the child then to mature himself if he has no inspiration from which to draw? The child, too, will grow to adulthood, still with childish beliefs, but outwardly projecting the appearance of a man.

31

Those who make child rearing the project of their lives are doing little more than any wild boar, rabbit, or insect might do —necessary to be sure, but hardly an endeavor that requires the dedication of a lifetime. More often than not a man's influence on his children is to harm them, but even his positive influence is somewhat negligible and limited. He's more likely to inspire another man's child than his own.

32

A child does not reach maturity through discipline but by the example set for him. This is why mankind is so generally immature.

33

Maturity is neither the burdening oneself with responsibilities nor the throwing off of fantasy. Rather it is the recognition of the complexities of the universe and the refusal to ignore unpleasant truths. It is, in a sense, relinquishing the protective coat of comfort and contentment in order to gain a greater understanding through a change in perspective.

34

The fiscal conservative is generally a prudent man while the social conservative is usually a prude.

35

A man is more a slave to his own perceptions and ideas than he is ever chained by the force of government (itself a perception of man).

36

Society can be merely one of man's many distractions.

37

The acquisition of societal power gives merely the illusion of flourishing.

38

Mandated education will always be little more than subjugation and control since mankind will always prefer to revel in its ignorance rather than suffer the pangs of understanding.

39

The more a society adopts the masculine perspective, the less civilized and cultured it will be.

40

The masculine exists to protect the feminine, not to dominate it. The warrior is never meant to rule since he is ill-equipped for such a task — as has been evidence throughout the course of human history.

41

When will mankind ever learn that tyranny is never just — no matter how well intentioned are its aims nor under what name it claims to wield its power? The more insidious tyranny arises from the subtle dominations of people in the name of freedom.

42

Too often man defines justice according to his own prejudices.

43

A man, like a child, will often cry "unfair" to that which does not serve to his advantage more often than he will use it as a declaration of injustice. In fact, he best understands injustice as a state of individual disadvantage.

44

Only a child is forgiven for his fundamentalism. The rest are stunted creatures whose value to the world is little more than as an evil which must be struggled against and overcome.

45

Politics will forever be plagued by the diseases that infect human nature. Unless man perfects himself he will never perfect his institutions.

46

The egalitarian makes the mistake of assuming that every man is able and willing to rule himself.

47

Suicide is not that difficult to comprehend. The curious question is why it appears to occur so infrequently. Perhaps because men have long ago relinquished their lives to some other form of suicide.

48

The law-abiding man secretly envies the courage of the criminal. He wishes that he, too, could shrug off the conventions of society and live only according to his own fancy. His resentment of criminality and his want to inflict the harshest of punishments upon the felon is rooted in this most secret jealousy.

49

Rousseau's idea of a "noble" savage is ludicrous. A man must, of course, sacrifice certain freedoms on the altar of society. These sacrifices enable him to lift himself above his baser, brutish nature and enjoy the more subtle aspects of cultivation and culture. The noble savage meanwhile is only noble if he remains completely isolated from other people who might otherwise serve to bring out the brute in him. Even in total isolation though, he appears less of a noble and more of a child — immature, unsophisticated, prone to tantrums and other extremes. Ignorance and nobility are hardly synonymous with one another.

50

A man may only feel truly free when, to a certain degree, his liberty is restricted. Otherwise he can find himself the victim of his passions.

51

"Freedom!" is the rally cry of children who still believe that such a thing exists as an overall totality. Freedom is always a freedom *from* something in particular and usually leads to a new restraint as a consequence.

52

Paternalism is man's arrogant belief in governing others while he remains woefully incapable of governing himself.

53

A man will choose between the gas chamber and being smothered in his sleep and he will call this freedom. While he was free to choose from the two alternatives, it is precisely this limitation on his choices that so troubles him in the first place.

54

In matters of politics, it is a good rule that one choose the path in opposition to the religious man.

55

Modern man is a slave to the marketplace, having long ago bartered his soul for a handful of "magic" beans.

56

In this shallow and wisdom-less age even a child can appear a sage.

57

The differences between totalitarianism and capitalism are minute with respect to domination and power. The former is overtly repressive while the latter is more subtle. The fundamental difference would be that capitalism allows one to choose his master from an established list of approved possibilities.

58

The modern industrial centuries shall provide very little for the next to value as anything but a passing curiosity. It shall become over time the new Middle Ages, assuming mankind survives at all.

59

"Set a goal" say the men of commerce and career "and soon you will achieve it. Or at the very least achieve enough to set another. These are the tenets of the successful man!" Bah! These are trophies which the dying man gazes upon on his death bed to convince himself that his was not a wasted life. He will die having missed the mark yet believing himself to be a marksman. "Attention must be paid to him!" cries the widow of salesman Willy Loman — if not but for the sake that you avoid his pathetic fate.

60

There may soon come a time when a man lives out the entirety of his adult existence without ever having met another soul except by way of some technological means. In this manner, mankind may become extinct long before he has been banished from the planet.

61

Man has taken life and made her a slave and in doing so he, the supposed master, has indentured himself to the role of watch keeper. For life will never stay in chains without constant surveillance and attention.

62

Given that the vast majority of men are, at best, children and, at worst, the most vicious of the animals, it seems somewhat logical to erect a state that would serve as a parent or master of this unruly bunch. Yet, such a parent or master is likely to be appointed from among just those people who need guidance the most. In other words, from within the ranks of children and beasts will emerge an alpha male or female to lead them. Such a leader, however, can only maintain the status quo or wield his scepter with vicious authority. The best leader would be chosen from among the outcasts of the herd. Yet, such a man is unlikely to desire such a position and even less likely to be asked to accept it. So, mankind is burdened with the reality that the people are being led, at best, by one of their own, more experienced, siblings or, at worst, by one of the most vicious creatures on earth. The mature man, the man of character and wisdom, is left to grapple with such a hoard of fools and live the life that suits his better nature. Luckily, this struggle also helps to develop such a man's spirit.

63

The social contract is forged into the mind of every child through parental rule and socialization. Let there be no mistake that this is the primary motive for public education — indoctrination. Everywhere the child travels in society, he is provided with interpretations of a text, the social contract, which he does not understand but eventually comes to accept as law. No man ever gives his free consent to such a contract. Rather he has been trained from birth to grant its legitimacy.

64

Of the many chains that a man may wear, the most revolting are those he fashions for himself — especially when he adorns them around his neck like jewelry.

65

All exchanges of personal goods for money share the characteristic of prostitution — selling that which is most intimate to oneself (one's labor, one's life) for a price, instead of giving it freely. If you are going to morally assign blame to the one you must chastise the other as well.

66

The poor of heart, mind, or spirit are generally parasitic to any society, but they are naturally so and, like the parasites of nature, they necessarily exist in a symbiotic relationship to their host. The outcome of disease for any particular society depends less upon the existence of the parasite and more upon the vitality and resistance of the host — an all around strong and lively host can feed the parasite for its entire lifetime without contacting so much as a sniffle.

67

For the most part, anytime the masses are given a voice you can expect that it will be shrill, vulgar, unintelligent and uninformed. If you deny them a voice, you can expect their leaders to be the same.

68

Every so often the mass of men engage in such a blatant act of injustice that the higher man must involve himself in order to maintain his own moral integrity. Yet, for the most part, he must withdraw from the hoard of men who consistently and forever engage in a litany of injustices large and small. Otherwise, he would do nothing but intervene and leave the bulk of his projects untouched.

69

Compulsory education for all merely leads to a partially educated citizenry since most care little for the knowledge they happen to acquire and will cease the task when the law releases them from this constraint. Yet, a partially educated citizen is more dangerous than one who can barely write his name because he believes he knows something.

70

Society only values the soldier for his utility. It writes him songs, poems and plays in order to deceive him into believing that he will somehow join the immortals for the sacrifice of his life. Parades are thrown in his honor and statues erected to his magnificence, all in the hopes of generating more recruits to the ranks of the expendable pawn. There is no honor, however, in naiveté.

71

The least effective form of tyranny is force. Belief is far more insidious.

72

Without religion to parent him, man turns to politics and the law. Yet, he shall no more find a heaven on earth than he shall find it in the sky.

73

The religious man often turns to politics in order to command others to conform to his religion. The irreligious man often turns to politics as a religion itself.

74

Everywhere one looks finds man searching for his parents. The state then serves as the father to such a child and must necessarily remain so as long as the child refuses to mature.

75

To tell a man born into poverty, with little in the way of intellectual capacity, that every opportunity is afforded to him as is available to the dullard born of wealth and privilege is the great lie of the religion of equality. Even if it were possible to make equal the financial status of these two types of men, they would still be lacking in natural abilities. The priests of equality would retort that each man is at least equal in opportunity as every other man similarly situated in natural capacities, but even that is a lie since no two people are similarly situated in natural ability in exactly the same manner. The priests may then reply that equality is an ideal for which to strive and in the attempt to achieve it mankind will make things more equitable and fair for himself. Yet, hierarchy exists everywhere in the ordering of nature. Does man believe that he is the one true exception? Hierarchy is established almost entirely by a certain amount of moral luck. What man "deserves" is, more often than not, something that he has lucked into. For any society to remain ordered it must insist that each of its citizens play their established role. Tyranny in some form is the modus operandi of any collective.

76

The virtuous and honorable man will be honorable and virtuous in any society in which he finds himself.

77

The more solitude a man needs and desires, the greater the man. Society, however, determines the greatness of a man in inverse order.

78

No one but the simplest of souls truly views the raising of children as a great accomplishment. Deep in the recesses of their subconscious, most people suspect that they are more likely to negatively affect the outcome of their child's personality than they might positively influence it.

79

Even the higher man lives within a society, not because he desires it, but because he must. He is social only insofar as he is required to be to survive.

80

The task of striving for social justice and human rights is similar to the efforts of the Dutch boy who runs to plug the leaking dyke with his finger. He quickly discovers that he must keep rushing to new places in the structure where fresh leaks have begun to spring.

81

There are many who flee to the forests in the hopes of escaping the tyranny of society only to find themselves slaves to different forces.

82

The people need to cease hailing the warrior as a hero if they wish to see the end of war.

83

It is perhaps naïve to believe that the majority of men shall ever purge the warrior from their hearts — it being his only means of expression. Therefore, let the women rule and use the men as merely guardians, humpbacked beasties that they are — unless they should prove themselves as something more significant than a human moat.

84

Trust no one who desires to be a leader of men since such a man wishes to associate almost exclusively with followers.

85

The greatest sin of industrialization has been in its granting greater power to those who are undeserving of it. The fool with a gun in his hand is far more dangerous than the one wearing a hat of bells.

86

The philosophy of tolerance and love has no answer for the Nazi and his kin — at least none that will entirely convince a man's intuition on the matter.

87

The difficulty that America shall face for all its existence is the fact that social organization is inherently unequal. Communism learned this lesson itself a few years back..

88

The idea that one creates his own destiny is a particularly American idiocy that stems from his over-inflated sense of self and the idea that destiny is something solely determined by material success.

89

Gold is a more valuable commodity to man because he finds it more appealing than feces. Yet, each have the same inherent worth — only man gives more import to the one over the other and he does so because he is fond of things that sparkle.

90

A man owns nothing but his soul. His property, possessions, family, friends, and animals are only his, as Rousseau suggests, insofar as he might be able to convince himself and others that he should have any right to them whatsoever. He doesn't share these "possessions" with all of humanity either since that, too, assumes a kind of rightful ownership by collective man. Yet, man is unlikely to abandon his notion of property and possession because he uses it as a means to assess his worth and assert his superiority over death. Unfortunately for him, the more he amasses materials as a means to display his merit, the less he seems to have of it.

91

The state, by its very nature, is inhuman and mechanical. It was designed as a device to create and keep order among a diverse and disparate collection of men, programmed to run as efficiently as possible according to a few set ideological commands. It should be no surprise that those who sit in the driver's seat of the machine can do little to steer its course.

92

Give nothing of yourself to the state but that which it demands for mere subsistence. Pledge it only hollow loyalties and echo its mantras only in defense of your life. Above all, be ready to abandon it entirely should it choose to become too much of a tyrant. It must and should intrude upon your freedom to the degree that it justly serves the needs of all its citizens, but it has no right to ask for your humanity as a kind of sacrificial lamb.

93

The ultimate sin of industrialization is that it failed to take humanity with it on its journey forward.

94

The suburb is a city with no center — quite indicative of its inhabitants.

95

If a man kills another it is in order to demonstrate his superiority, his spiritual supremacy over and above his enemy. The society then who finds him guilty and sentences him to punishment is engaged in the same ancient game, only theirs is to show the supremacy of the state and by extension all of its citizens. In this manner, nationalism is born and lives to breed an untold brood of murderers.

96

Mankind is much more interested to see its youth grow to be useful members of society than to be fully realized human beings — supposing, I guess, that you cannot accomplish the latter without the former first. A subtle ruse played upon the slaves by their master.

97

The industrial age is destined to be forgotten — a time of human history, like the Middle Ages, when humanity lost its collective mind. It will be the void between the greater epochs that posterity ponders, if any remain, and wonders if humanity existed there.

98

"Civilized" man, that is to say, the "good" citizen, is taught to murder softly, bloodlessly.

99

Feminism is nothing but another example of the glorification of materialism — the greater power being sold out to the lesser for a little more comfort and contentment, equality and fairness. Yet, the real problem is not that women are paid less than men or that they have less in the way of economic opportunity. The true crisis is that the world values and glorifies those qualities that are predominately masculine, exactly those qualities that are so superficial and destructive. To create and nurture one's soul into a formation of "divine" character is the highest achievement possible for man, and these are chiefly feminine characteristics. A truly worthwhile feminism would be aimed at ceasing the glorification of masculine values such as force, conquest, violence, ignorance, and stupidity.

100

It is of no little significance that the advent of the cartoon and its popularity are mostly a modern phenomenon. After all, man has made a caricature of himself in the industrial age. He has simplified himself into basic lines and one dimensional attitudes and made for himself an art form to reflect these elements of his nature.

101

Beware of the wolf you've tamed as a pet for he still has that trace of wild blood within him. Be alert. He can lash out at the slightest provocation and without any reason. Where then will be your notions of equality and justice? Where will fly your beliefs in culture and refinement? They will lie bleeding on the grassy floor of nature — the place where all of man's inventions must go to pray and sacrifice that they not be leveled by the wind. You may take revenge on the caged bear who rips apart and devours the unwitting toddler that wanders into his pen, but it is the parents who are to blame for the child's demise.

102

Is it possible that love between two people is nothing nobler than any other social conformity and should rank no higher to man's "greatness" quotient than paying his taxes or tipping his waitron?

103

Be wary of the hates of state or any mass of men. For what they hate as a group, is you — unless you should choose to join them.

104

The greater the mass of men that constitute a majority, the simpler must be the question of which they are called upon to decide.

105

Humanity may have tamed the animals, but they have made savage the man.

106

A great society is born despite its politicians and is often set to ruin because of them.

107

Take heed that the suit you wear to your job does not become your skin.

108

Psychotherapy does not intend to cure, but to normalize. It is the science of mediocrity.

109

The disadvantaged in any society will usually complain that they are limited to what they can achieve. They either lack resources or opportunity and they wish to have the same access to succeed in life as everyone else. This is, of course, a perfectly reasonable request and one that any government should work to help realize. Yet, utopias are few and far between in this world of sensation and experience. There will always exist the advantaged and the disadvantaged in the world of material assets. Thus, it is better to value those things which are immaterial and seek to take possession of *them*. The economically disadvantaged are troubled because of their faulty perceptions, not because they lack the means to secure a meaningful life. They unthinkingly accept the pathetic values of their society. Their pain and frustration then stems from the fact that they have acquired the same illusion as their more advantaged contemporaries, but are unable to fulfill it. Should they choose to abandon this illusion and seek instead to acquire more valuable virtues than property and possession —more noble, human virtues — they would begin to view themselves as among the richest of souls and those that they once envied would seem to them then as pitiful and worthy only of tears. Of course, some might protest that such thinking seeks merely to keep the disadvantaged in a state of weak acceptance of their fate, controlled and mollified by the state and the wealthier men who are further advantaged by such appeasement. This is most likely true. The man who chooses not to play a particular game is surely at a disadvantage to win. Yet, it is the game itself that the higher man would find unappealing as well as an unworthy use of the little time he should spend on the earth. The rest can do as they inevitably will.

110

When politics begin to slip from the lips, one's brain begins to drain from the ears.

111

A government should be made to favor the exceptional, not the common, perspective.

112

A true revolution ensues when perceptions are changed. Political revolution merely forces carnage.

113

America was a great idea that was conceived of genius and ruined by the more common elements of man.

114

A society cannot logically justify the outlaw of prostitution with the acceptance of a service industry.

115

The destructive component of communism or tyranny is that the individual is sacrificed for the benefit of society. In capitalism or democracy, the situation is reversed; the destructive element is that society is sacrificed for the sake of the individual. Nature would scoff at such crude and extreme methods of social organization.

116

Democracy engenders a similar effect as that of a sickly patient who must go on trial in order for a jury of accountants to decide what is wrong with him.

117

The people of a free nation must of necessity wear their own restraints or, as Nietzsche suggests, they will inevitably wear the restraints of another.

118

The culture of capitalism is so controlled by the compulsion for money that every day it trades the futures of mankind and life itself on the market as if they were mere commodities.

119

The politicians will not save a dying society for they are as much carriers of the disease as are the vast majority of the citizens. The only governmental solution is tyranny which will not provide a cure, of course, but will at least superficially save the patient — stabilizing the vital signs while the vitality dies away.

120

While it's true, as has been claimed, that liberalism is Christ without the cross, it is equally true that conservatism is the force which nailed him to it.

121

The man who champions "freedom" above all else is often he who fatefully sows the seeds for tyranny.

122

Man is not, as Aristotle believed, a political animal by nature. He is, instead, a political animal merely by circumstance.

123

Modern man searches for his new God, his truer world, his escape from the harsh realities of existence, through his newfound belief in political utopia. There, he reasons, will life finally succumb to his concepts of moral perfection.

124

Society idolizes the individual only in so far as his individuality serves the interests of the collective. This is why so many great men have gone unnoticed in their own time.

125

When men finally begin to view the warrior as less of a self-sacrificing, egoless creature and more of a deluded and manipulated toy at the mercy of the machine, then will wars become less populated with so many willing corpses. Rarely do boys die in the actual defense of their nation and more frequently are they sent to slaughter for the superficial ideologies of their fathers. The warrior is not so much a protector as he is a diplomatic chess piece sacrificed by another for the sake of the queen.

126

How quickly do those born to wealth and privilege take up the flag of meritocracy and proudly fly its colors above their garrison, as if they have earned some kind of victory by virtue of their being born to the winning side. They believe that they somehow deserve their status through the labor of their mothers. It never occurs to them that merit is awarded not with gold or silver, for those are the derivatives of luck and circumstance, but by the richness of character. If they had been born into a society that placed no value on capital, they would suddenly perceive themselves as pathetic individuals indeed since this is their natural state.

127

It often becomes the case that the more power a man acquires over others, the less he will be a master of himself — time and energy being both of limited quantity.

128

The parenting of children is a way to test the merits of a man's character. It may also serve to contribute, under certain conditions, to the *development* of character.

129

Beware the fear monger for he wishes to enslave in the same manner in which he has become enslaved himself. It is, after all, more comforting to walk in chains with others than to walk with them alone. He has a love of drama and spectacle and will fabricate them in his mind where he does not find them in his world. It consumes him to such a degree that he sees himself as a kind of heroic figure, leading the resistance against whichever enemy he wishes to imbue with fearful qualities. He is, at heart, a coward, of course, because he is ultimately frightened of everything and unwilling to face it alone.

130

Freedom is not a goal in itself but merely a means to some other, more significant, end. In this manner, freedom is not the ultimate value, but often merely a necessary condition to achieve what is truly valuable to a man. There is no need for absolute freedom as long as one's vital aims are able to be satisfied. The problem is that man often believes he should be free to seek anything he desires while the religious or patriotic fool would have him pursue only one avenue to the good life.

131

A tyrant is essentially a coward, whether he impels others to kill and silence his rivals, or performs the deed himself. In each case he proves himself to possess a weaker soul than even a petty criminal. In the first instance, he hasn't the nerve to perform the act by his own hand and though in the last he may seem a more courageous beast, at least having the bravado to undertake the deed, he still remains too fragile a creature to live in a world in which his enemy resides. The tyrant concedes defeat in the worldly arena by banishing his foe to another realm from where he will never return. Yet, while he may have purged the man from existence, he will be unable to contend with the form into which such a man, and others like him, will eventually change.

132

Society exists as a means to artificially cultivate and control those souls, the great majority, who find the task impossible to accomplish themselves. For those fools who think it appropriate to express every feeling in their breast or actualize every passion that arises from their soul, society stands as a kind of sentry to protect the rest of humanity. In this sense it does serve as a kind of necessary parental influence. It only errs when it continues to exert its authority over those few who have managed to sufficiently mature and are no longer in need of the nest.

133

The higher man is not disturbed by the "masks" that he must don from time to time while out in public any more than it bothers him that he should be clothed. He understands the need for it and is not concerned with those childish and superficial notions of freedom which promote the ridiculous creed that one should not be restrained in much of anything. Freedom is, for the higher man, something closer to a state of mind than a fact of nature.

134

A man's culture, no doubt, helps to shape the construct of a man, however, a man, too, helps shape his culture. Yet, if the culture fails in the first instance to properly cultivate an artistic perspective into its devotees, it will quickly suffer from stagnation due to a dearth of competent sculptors that might have otherwise breathed new life into her.

135

Man often congratulates himself that he has essentially eradicated slavery from the world when what he has accomplished instead is to merely change its form — chiefly into economic slavery. Poverty still makes slaves of all kinds of souls, but with the added illusion that their servitude is somehow freely chosen and the deluded belief that, with enough hard work, such an individual can rise above their blighted state. In this manner man has abdicated himself from the responsibility of slavery while continuing to directly benefit from its effects. Yet, we should not overlook those fools who *do* willingly sell themselves into chains in order to satisfy more self-indulgent desires than the necessities of food or shelter, those who would do the bidding of any master that might provide riches, fame, or possessions.

136

Justice is merely the law, a social construction that is collectively agreed upon and can thus be collectively changed. Even cannibalism or any other such presently considered squeamish act can be considered as having a part in justice should enough people agree to it. Justice merely exists to facilitate group cohesion. Yet, this is not a fatal flaw to its value or subsistence. Mankind resists the artificial ordering of society on the grounds that it is contrived and arbitrary, not consisting of some more natural and eternal base. In so doing, he conspires to create yet another contrivance — that of natural or eternal law. Yet, he will never free himself of artificial ordering and one can only hope that he begins to realize that these kinds of arrangements are actually part of his greatness — his imagination in creating meaning and value for his world. Yet, he remains rigidly fearful that anything then might be permitted if he allows for change to be a part of the system (forgetting, of course, that human sentiments only gradually adjust). This inflexibility ultimately ends up chipping loose something of that order which is fundamentally necessary to its construction, thereby causing it to flow back into chaos again.

137

In order to perpetuate a true sense of fairness, justice must be concerned with the weakest members of a society first. The rich man might cry that it is unjust to tax him at a higher rate than the man who has little, but the flaw in his thinking is his belief that he somehow *deserves* his money — conveniently forgetting the lucky advantages that procured the stuff for him in the first place. He vastly overestimates the effects of hard work in an unjust society.

138

The only political organization that is "natural" to man is a ranking of the strong over the weak. This is his natural, animal state. Yet, the glory of man, that which at times rises him above his innately beastly self, is that he improves, beautifies, and sublimates the brute reality of his condition and creates something altogether new. He operates within two dimensions then, the natural and the artificial, which cannot be reconciled with one another. The first is his more "authentic" state while the other is — or can be anyway — an aspect of his better self.

139

The problem in the hierarchy of a "free" society is that a man will often position himself — through guile, accident, or deceit — to a rank for which he does not belong. Soon enough these little awkward and unfortunate rankings lead to the destruction of the entire structure of society as a whole. The Omega wolf who is given charge of the pack quickly enough brings about their starvation.

140

Wielding power over others is merely man's pathetic attempt to gain some small advantage over his own life. He intuitively believes that this kind of power will allow him to rule over his own mortality. However, control and power eventually lead again to chaos as something as vital as life and volatile as the human being will not remain constrained for long and the man of power will be forced to helplessly chase after his minions to ensure that they behave — a task that will ultimately become far too all-consuming. Ironically, the more influence and control that one attempts to exact over his life, the more unstable it becomes.

141

A man puts himself in chains more often than his society restrains him and in shackles more binding and constrictive than were ever forged by the circumstances of his birth.

142

The vast majority of men need to be dragged along the path of justice since they possess no inclination to travel it themselves. Yet, the only man that would attempt to undertake such a feat is the politician who, being a fool himself and utterly lacking in understanding as to what justice entails, will only lead men along the path of his own prejudices.

143

Even the best form of government ever conceived may fall to ruin by being drawn to any of the many extremes.

144

The reason the Holocaust and so many other atrocities like it are so unfathomable to the modern mind is that modern man does not conceive of his contemporaries as being essentially vicious, aggressive, and susceptible to the will of others. Like children, the majority of men need, even crave, the dictator, for only he can bring discipline and order to the chaos of their heart — a feat they are unable to complete themselves. They bleat for freedom while they secretly chaw for the authoritarian to return to them. The rigorous disciplinarian, however, is just as corrupt, vicious, and destructive as are they.

145

The essential problem with all theories of social contract is not that they assume people to be self-interested, but the assumption that people are rational in deducing their interests.

146

A man may blame society for the necessity of his having to conform to its demands and mindlessly follow its rather arbitrary and superficial rituals, but he is ultimately responsible for this state. His feeling of need that he must conform and serve is a choice that he decides upon as a means to keep him safe from ridicule. Yet, he must come to realize that escaping the ridicule of his contemporaries does not free him from suffering the ridicule of his own conscience.

147

Every man should have a fundamental right to his own ignorance and stupidity. However, he does not possess the right to loose this stupidity upon the world in the form of laws and politics since these domains should be ruled by the more estimable qualities of education and reason.

148

There is nothing wrong with wealth, religion, power or distraction in and of themselves. The great man wields such goods with admirable success, although rarely is he ever concerned with wealth and power. Yet, for the lesser man, these furnishings seem to warp his ego to a disproportionate degree and fixate his desire on things unworthy of such obsessive attention. The lesser man then finds it impossible to see the forest for the trees and entirely loses his way in the woods.

149

It is interesting to note that the advocates for anarchy are quite often those whose build, intellect, and character are such that they would suffer most from an absence of law and order.

150

Men believe that by altering their government they can somehow eliminate the tragic nature of life itself, but the suffering is due to his lack of perspective. It is not poverty, disease, destruction and death that are the ultimate evils that a man must face, but instead his perception of these obstacles. The great man finds no varying degree of significance to his life because it is played out in poverty or wealth, in sickness or in health. His perspective is such that he views these things as trivial and to a large extent outside the realm of his control. Imprisoned or free to wander at will, his focus will be the same — to understand the complexity and virtues of his character and improve upon them.

151

Man is everywhere fighting for his political freedom from the indignity of oppression. Yet, rarely will he struggle to unyoke the chains that are forged together by his own self-perception.

152

The only place a man is truly free is in his soul, the mind being too entrenched within the boundaries of its genetic code. There are, of course, varying degrees of external restraint. After all, there can be no such thing as society without some form of restriction on a man's liberty — all such restrictions being severe to one extent or another. Yet, the government that man seems to prefer is the one wherein he can imagine himself to *believe* that he is free.

153

The failed experiment with individualism in America is going to entail a draconian response to finally curtail it, given that the individuals themselves will no longer be able to control that wild beast of liberty that they have irresponsibly unleashed and allowed to run amok within their hearts. This will be the final shame and irony of America: that it gleefully and willingly consents for its inmates to freely run the asylum, but when these same patients prove to be unsuitable to the task, it will ultimately choose to force them into submission again.

154

Utilitarianism is the moral system of democracy — pragmatically effective, despite all of its morally questionable conclusions, primarily because it focuses on the concerns of the majority and as such enjoys rigorous support from the greater mass of men. Yet, even tyranny rationalizes that its dreadful rule is for the benefit of the majority. Perhaps it's time to cease requesting the opinions of the majority in matters of great importance and instead begin to consider the perspectives of the wise.

155

If it is true that religion is the opiate of the masses, then so too is politics.

156

A man is only chained to the extent that he allows himself to be. Since the soul is always free, its restraint is within the control of each individual and they have the final determination as to whether their souls are to be enslaved. That is not to say that external forces can't influence this decision through the infliction of pain or some other spiritually taxing procedure. Yet, even the man in the most wretched state of external restraint — locked away in the dark basement or chained to a wall or confined by physical tortures, the likes of which only mankind is able to conceive — can imagine himself heroically astride a caramel stallion on the way to Elysium.

157

The Greek notion of excellence is primarily formed by competition; that is, two or more opponents compete in feats of skill (sports, the arts, etc.), the winner of this competition then proves himself to be the most excellent. Some have even gone so far as to use this idea as a metaphor for all of life — life being a competition for a variety of resources and the one who acquires these goods is determined to be the winner or the most excellent. However, the problem with such a perspective, particularly in the arts, is that the judgment of excellence is determined by others who may or may not themselves be a wise or capable evaluator. It is better then to cultivate competition with oneself and learn to be a competent judge of one's own accomplishments and growth.

158

The nasty little truth about all societies is that its soldiers eventually die in vain, used as a plastic game piece in some political diversion designed to attain, establish, or otherwise broaden another man's power of influence. A comprehensive understanding and recognition of this particular fact about war might be able to curb warfare entirely.

159

The modern capitalist society and its religious equivalent, the fascist state, make kings of businessmen and priests — all of whom quickly prove woefully unworthy of the title.

160

War is not much of an atrocity for those who do not have to fight it. It is, instead, something of a game — an imaginary conflict that seeks to obliterate all opposition in the service of winning. To this end, the soldier, the civilian, and the enemy are all stripped of their humanity and molded into plastic figurines that can be manipulated along the game board.

161

Bureaucracy, by its very nature, is inhuman.

162

Modern society is, by design, concerned with the external and superficial since it evolved in order to address purely practical issues of organization, coordination, and material prosperity. Man's "alienation" from this particular kind of social order has nothing whatsoever to do with the society itself being somehow corrupt. The fact that the industrial culture arose at a time when the belief in religion began to wane significantly points to the cause for the birth of the modern state itself — as an answer to meaninglessness. Yet, that which remains solely on the surface will almost always fail to sprout roots. Thus, the modern man finds that his life is lacking depth.

163

Men seem to have surrendered the task of improving upon themselves and are instead intent on perfecting society, hoping that some kind of institutional structure will eliminate the struggles, sorrows, and inequities of life.

164

"Stability at almost any cost" is the plea of the lesser man. He is unwilling to acknowledge the fact of nature that change is an inevitable and necessary aspect of life itself. It is those who wish for an inflexible and superficial structure to their existence, those of the weakest character, who advocate on behalf of tradition, fascism, and tyranny in all its many guises. For them, such institutions provide a safe haven, even in its most brutal forms, from the fluid and evolving motion of life. They are the enemies of thought, the enemies of the human. They are the fundamentalists of all the world's religions and nations. It is they who should be opposed in their every venture; ignored at every turn. Yet, it is also they who will propose war as a kind of stabilizing force since force is their only weapon. They have no recourse to wisdom and self-control.

11

The State of the Spirit

1

The "average man" has constructed his society as a distraction against his own responsibility toward awareness. The majority, ensconced within their own laziness and cowardice, fashion elaborate schemes to buffer themselves against what should be the primary goal of their lives — the fruition and exaltation of their own depths; to make conscious that to which nature may only dream. Instead, they divert their attention to the acquisition of wealth, romance, and experience. They celebrate the attainment of normalcy. They wallow in the muddy pits of their potential and respond that this is their genius. Theirs, they claim, is an overwhelming talent for the mundane, the horrific, the ridiculous, or the inconsequential; as if we are to believe that what exists within the deepest recesses of their soul is nothing more than something trite and superficial.

2

The biggest question that arises in a man's life, the question that usurps all others in scope, magnitude, significance, and profundity, remains: How should one live that best exemplifies the greatness of this creature known as "man?" How shall I set the example?

3

At the end of Death of a Salesman, Arthur Miller has his character demand that attention must be paid to the poor Willy Loman who wanted only to be liked. Why should attention be paid to such a pathetic creature other than as an omen to others that they should not waste their lives with pettiness and thus themselves suffer such a miserable fate?

4

The goal of life is not death but how best to die — as a fine example — and few will die well who did not first live that way.

5

All that does not inspire kills.

6

A man will often treat animals poorly because he secretly knows that they naturally possess more integrity than he.

7

The goal of the higher man is not the benefit of his actions for mankind; however, this is often the result.

8

Those who have something important to accomplish would be best advised to steer clear of any and all forms of suicidal distraction.

9

Physical gratifications and delights rank among the highest of all pleasures to only those souls who are so common that they know nothing of joys that transcend the physical entirely — the aesthetic/creative/intellectual pleasures. The greater mass of men, after all, much prefer music to which they can dance rather than a composition which engages more than simply the Dionysian beast within them.

10

How does one live one's life with the knowledge that chaos rules the universe, meaning is meaningless, and that existence is, in its very essence, ultimately futile — with delusion, pretense, forgetfulness, or Courage?

11

Men seem to always attempt to perfect humanity by superficial means, manipulating the physical or environmental factors that might influence him to better himself. The only way to truly change humanity is from within. This is accomplished by inspiration. If one is inspired by something, he cannot help but change. If he is inspired to greatness, he may not achieve greatness, but he will at least be significantly improved by the stretching of his spirit.

12

It is the temptation of science to dispute the "reality" of anything that cannot be either seen or measured. Yet, it is precisely those things which cannot be measured that measure the worth of a man.

13

When a soul is no longer immersed in becoming and instead has settled into the contentment from his being at the present moment, he ceases to be authentically human. Authenticity is an elastic state of becoming in such a way that changes him mostly for the better. Inauthenticity is either the static state of a soul at rest for too long or one that is becoming in decay.

14

There are only three types of souls in existence: 1) the great soul, 2) the animal soul, and 3) the brutish soul — listed in their order of significance

15

It should be as easy to tame the spirit of a wolf as tame the spirit of a man. Yet, more often than not, the spirit of the man proves to be the least resistant to domestication.

16

A man's intuition, at least a well developed intuition that is given its due attention, is a better guide to the good life than is his reason. Instead of attempting to become objectively dispassionate and reasonable about his choices or decisions in life, a man should consult his intuitions. This is dangerous, of course, because man, being imperfect, will often mistake his passions for his intuition, thinking intuition to be merely the opposite of reason. The intuition, however, is the mediator between reason and passion. It is only irrational in the sense that it makes decisions, at times, which do not make sense to reason. Yet, if both reason and the passions have been developed and cultivated accordingly, intuition is the highest form of intellect in that it incorporates the whole of man's being — it *is* the spiritual.

17

It is not a child's innocence that connects him to the spirit of the world, but his imagination and curiosity. The adult laments his loss of innocence, but gives little attention to his abandonment of these two more significant attributes of the child.

18

Man's spirit cannot be justified by reasoning. One encounters it intuitively, much like a work of art — reflecting on it, studying it, perhaps trying to reason in order to explain it to another. However, it is ultimately something that one *feels* to be true. The easier it might be explained, the less profound are its dimensions.

19

It is inspiration, more than anything else, which fuels the human spirit.

20

Often one comes to expect a certain dourness to arise from maturation, but dourness is not a sign of maturation or developing sophistication but of the man-child growing old.

21

All men should seek to develop an artistic soul.

22

The soul itself is nothing but a feeling and an idea about the nature of one's character.

23

Repression is not refinement.

24

The more time a man spends in contemplation, the more he tames the beast within his soul.

25

All that is not contemplation is oftentimes merely distraction. Man is at his most authentic in the act of contemplation — that engagement with the world through the process of perceiving, reflecting, and interpreting in the hopes of better understanding one's own existence. All human greatness arises from it — philosophy, art, religion, and morality.

26

The cultivation of the spirit should be the goal of any man.

27

The masculine subjugates while the feminine cultivates. Therefore, one should cultivate the feminine aspects of their soul.

28

As Shakespeare divined, all the world is but a stage. The job of each player is to perfect the presentation of his character and do his very best to live his part in service to the play itself. If he should truly wish to know the play, he will need to read it in its entirety, study it in his spare time, and contemplate its significance as a work of art. Otherwise, whether he possesses a leading role or is merely a small player in the drama, he will have gained nothing much when the curtain drops.

29

One who looks inside himself and sees little to admire is confronted with a challenge which he will either courageously accept through a commitment to better himself or forlornly decline by distracting himself with pity and forgetting.

30

There is little doubt that human life is psychologically motivated by a will to power. Those who deny this are thinking of power from the narrow perspective of political power or domination of other individuals, but these are only external, negative manifestations of power. Power from a broader, and more appropriate, perspective is the surge of the force of life, of vitality. Power is not always violent and destructive. Witness the child attempting to increase an advantage over his father or trying any number of primitive means to gain control of his world and flourish. The power that is best to cultivate, however, is the feeling of power that one can derive from within. This kind of power is immune to external political coercion or the forces of fate. It does not bow to a man's occupation, his financial status, the opinion of his contemporaries, or the accomplishments for which he may or may not be credited. It is the power of the higher man, the mature individual — he that can find himself in any situation and remain feeling as potent as a king.

31

Passion rules the child like an unrelenting monster — it so rules the man-child as well.

32

Contentment is a hallmark of mediocrity.

33

No man can concern himself with matters of the soul when his stomach is empty and his bed is atop a rock. Only religion is possible for such a man — or food and shelter.

34

Knowing oneself only arises when one has come to learn about others. They serve as a means to compare and contrast one's own thoughts and feelings and thus become conscious of them.

35

Many fools like to believe that they are building character when in fact they are merely constructing an external edifice that they then title: "Me." The construction of the self, however, is primarily built from within and requires a great number of years devoted to solitude and contemplation for it to stand to the world.

36

Many believe that wealth, fame, and political power have no value because they are not by nature permanent in any way. Instead, they lack value because they are external to the value-maker himself. Ultimately, they will always ring hollow for him because he seeks to value without that which he finds lacking within.

37

Hume was shrewd in pointing out that there is no "self" or "soul" because it cannot be identified in any empirical sense. Yet, the soul does exist, but as a complex system, not a singular empirical entity. The state, to reword Searle's example, is not its governing body, or its citizens, or its laws, or its culture, but a complex amalgamation of them all.

38

A man will take great pains to restore his honor and reputation, whether they be sullied unjustly or no, yet he will do little to correct the dishonor and ill repute that he has rightly judged to exist from within. In other words, men are more concerned if others judge them to be dishonorable than if they do so themselves.

39

A man will never discover his soul amid the light of day. He must walk along the streets or hills in the middle of the night while the din of the world is hushed and all the people are sleeping in their beds.

40

If the heart of a warrior could be sublimated into something more worthy, more noble, more beneficial to all mankind, he should see an end to war and the rise of culture.

41

To kill the warrior within one's own heart is the only truly noble war.

42

The ugliness found in the hearts of most men is almost too much to bear viewing — especially as it becomes noticeable within oneself.

43

Those who choose to ignore the darkness will never see the light.

44

The man who derives his power from external means (acquisition, wealth, fame, politics) will find himself at the mercy of elements that are beyond his control and he will quickly discover that all of his power can be taken from him in an instant. A hurricane can arise and swat his holdings to the ground; old age can remove him from his occupation; and he is brought to powerlessness immediately. A man who derives his power from within holds it with him until his death and only adds to it as he moves along the path of his life. His power is tied to the spiritual realm of the universe and while the work that he creates as a result of this inner power may crumble into dust, such works were merely external manifestations of what he possessed within. The crucial problem of modern man is that he derives his power from outside himself. He reads only to develop skills in order to build or to distract himself from his labors; he experiences in order to gain more wealth or fame; he prays in order to further his advantage on the competition; he contemplates in order to design something new; and he dies having possessed nothing of any value. He is a man who has discarded the pearl in favor of the oyster.

45

There is a significant feeling of power that is generated by exhibiting control over one's desires.

46

Transcendence is not an experience composed of any permanence; one does not transcend the earthly realm for all eternity (except in death). It is, instead, a quite fleeting experience whose import inspires a man to share some expression of it.

47

The individual soul itself is not immortal. It can merely participate in the immortal from time to time during its brief encounter with consciousness.

48

A man should model his spirit after the wolf — cautious and reserved, ravenous, trusting only in his pack, cunning, quiet, intelligent and prepared to devour all which may nourish him. Likewise, a man should be attuned to the howl of his soul, that beautiful moan, which is the foundation of all artistic endeavor.

49

What a gift is consciousness to one forsaken — taste to the salt sea, touch to the wet stone. What have you to offer the sun but these? What need have you in vanity and pride, in luxuries and religious minds? Your greatness lies far beyond such narrow measures. You must never allow the rusting of your soul.

50

It seems somehow cruel that men should grow old without the comfort of gaining wisdom.

51

Man views so many elements in the universe as something foreign to him. Such a man will always feel alienated to a certain extent, even if he is embraced by the majority of men. However, the man who can identify with all of creation will always feel strangely connected though he be an outcast to the world of men.

52

Oh, that the fates might pitch and strike your shape and throw your soul into constant turmoil, like the true lover burns amidst the flames, hardly seems a fortune to be fearful for one left numb to the coursing of his veins.

53

A man has as much responsibility to the possible manifestations of his future self as he does to his present one.

54

A man may alter the given facts about himself and "reinvent" himself anew, but these alterations merely cover up his true nature while, at the same time, revealing himself to be something of a coward.

55

Science and technology allow a man to alter certain given circumstances of his life, but they will not necessarily permit him to change the content of his character. Oftentimes, these alterations merely serve to confuse the issue to such a degree that a man cannot find his way back to himself.

56

A man of good character will never be so if his nature remains untested as to its merit. It must undergo the crucible of experience and the gauntlet of unworthy souls to both solidify and polish its significance.

57

A man does not so much choose his character as he affirms it through all of his choices.

58

A man does not feel anguish, as Sartre claims, because he has no foundation to support his choice of character — leaving aside the common man's puerile interpretation that man then has freedom to decide anything and everything for himself. His foundation, however, is his feeling, his intuition, that the choice he made was the correct one for him at the time. He is not a foundationless foundation; the decision does not derive from nothingness; it arrives from the fountainhead of each individual spirit. While a man cannot, of course, point to his spirit or understand it as some kind of concrete entity, he *feels* it to exist in the deepest recesses of his being. He will only experience anguish if his choices are lacking the support of this deeper region. To take on character traits that do not resonate within this secret well will inevitably lead a man to grief. He will be wearing garments that do not fit and he will most certainly find himself either tripping over them or struggling to breathe because they are too constricting.

59

If every man were to care only for the betterment of his own soul, and leave the rest alone to likewise care for their own, the collective would ultimately reap the benefits. Alas, one cannot rely on one's neighbors to undertake such a task, committed as they are only to the betterment of others.

60

When the modern man reads from Nietzsche that he should give style to his character, he immediately runs out to purchase a tie because he is so externally motivated and inclined to extroversion that he cannot conceive of style being anything other than some kind of outward show. Style, however, has to do with the beauty of one's spirit — one's own particular ethical disposition, perspective, understanding and wisdom. These are traits that may not immediately reveal themselves in the day to day humdrum reality of modernity. They relate to the dignity of a man and are sometimes only seen during moments of duress or some other extreme circumstance.

61

A man should never let himself be subjected to the fickleness of fortune, whether it be good fortune or bad, for he will quickly find himself bandied about by the forces of fate and circumstance and his own soul shall become like a stranger to him.

62

Wisdom is not cultivated overnight. It may be felt within as a budding flower, but it is the type of plant that is extremely delicate. It must be given time to fully bloom while great care is afforded to it. Its gardener must acquire a wealth of knowledge for its proper care and not be too impatient for it to grow. All the while, he must protect it from those assorted forces that seek its destruction.

63

All life is essentially, at its core, meaningless, devoid of purpose, reason, or morality. Thus, it is pointless, random, and absurd. Yet, the challenge for man is to *make* his life meaningful — to imbue it with purpose, reason, and morality. This entails much more than simply doing what pleases him. His being requires more than just the gratification of certain pleasures to be authentic and worthwhile. He is too complex to expect that he will accept a purpose for his life which does not permeate his entire existence, reasons that do not resonate with his character, or morality that is intuitively immoral. Any attempt to do so will eventually lead to some form of suicide.

64

A man must develop a sense of gratitude for his existence, for all existence, if he is to relate appropriately to the world. He must develop the poetic sensibility of recognizing the infinite depths and dimensions of life and welcome, while he can, the sheer divinity of the cosmos.

65

"God" *is* truly alive and well, but has yet to be discovered by the trifling narrowness of man's perception. "God" is beyond naming, but if she must be given gender, she would be no doubt received as feminine. One *feels* the presence of divinity; one does not possess knowledge of it. She is the God of the poets, not the philosophers, and certainly not the priests. She does not exist as the savior of man, that he must do for himself, but of creation. She provides no meaning to a man's life but engenders his gratitude and fills him with a profound feeling of significance.

66

The striving for wealth, reputation, or material power does not itself cause a man to be miserable; rather it is usually the miserable man who is drawn to these means because they appear, on the surface, to be elixirs for his malady.

67

A man is no more free to choose the characteristics of his own soul than he is able to choose the nature of the world in which he finds himself. His chore is to discover the better essence of his own character in relation to the world entire — beautifying, illuminating, and improving both in the process.

68

Philosophers often seem no wiser than their contemporaries, some even denouncing the idea of wisdom itself, because they still believe that such a condition as wisdom can be arrived at by reason alone.

188

69

Filling one's days with activity may relieve a man of his boredom, but it merely distracts him from the confrontation with its cause.

70

As it is in nature, the inner life of man is fundamentally chaotic with passions, feelings, beliefs and memory all clashing together to cause such a cacophony that it is a wonder a man can make any sense of it at all. Yet, he will, at least to a certain degree, begin to order and arrange things so as to make meaning of some of this material. He is always threatened though by undeveloped or unconscious elements rashly rising to the surface, overtaking him suddenly unawares. The task for the man of character is to cultivate, tame and utilize all of these rash, chaotic, and sometimes dangerous features of the soul, to control them for use at the appropriate time, if at all, and forge a higher meaning to his existence. Nature, though at its foundation chaotic, is ordered by balance and harmony and exhibits a sublime beauty as a result, so too should be the man of character.

71

Just as an actor "puts on" different roles and engages in a variety of circumstances on stage, there is a decided sameness to each of the characters that he portrays, an aspect of himself that remains, for the most part, growing but constant. This essence is his true character.

72

The self or soul is precisely that being in which all the fragmented experiences, memories, thoughts, beliefs, and feelings cohere and unify. The self is the order amidst the chaos of a man's inner world. It is an idea, a conception of unity brought about by the perception of connectedness to a vast array of differing data, threaded together by the mind and understood as this mysterious and quite necessary notion of the self.

73

Humor is a particular perspective that allows a man to reject the tyrannical seriousness of life. It permits him to rebel against even that which is most terrible in his existence. No man can be a true rebel without it.

74

Reflection is not a tool that one utilizes to discover their inner self. It is, instead, one of the most profound activities of a self (or part of one anyway) already discovered, a mode of being that informs all aspects of one's life. In contemplation, one convalesces with the divine nature of consciousness and begins to feel himself connected to something greater than his own individual soul. The absence of reflection makes him something of a beast.

75

Those who realize their dreams suffer from the stupor of self-satisfaction — giddy with the spoils of their achievements and delighted with power bestowed by the radiance of their own success. Such men may succeed in possessing all the world while never acquiring even a brief glimpse into their own spirit to discover the material of which it's made.

76

The sun rises anew each day with the hope of rousting man from his somnambulistic slumber and illuminating the beauty of the entire world to him. Yet, man has grown too accustomed to sleeping through the day and merely yawns at the approach of sun rise.

77

Every man daily chooses from a list of possibilities that arise largely without his consent and out of his control. His fate then unfolds not as some sort of overall conscious design but, essentially, as a product of happenstance. His reaction to the outcomes of his "choices" is what constitutes the narrative of his character. The child, for instance, may be offered the option of either walking off to bed or being carried there by his parents. In either case, bed is inevitable. The manner in which he arrives there is his decision. The child may choose to fight and scream at the injustice of his fate and rend his garments in wild, dramatic rebellion in the hope of swaying the decision of the gods, but ultimately his destiny has already been sealed and he is left to sadly weep himself to sleep. Another child, however, might choose to at least enjoy the dignity of walking himself to bed, accepting the conditions of his isolation until such a time as he might be relieved from them, even perhaps, if he is to be of such fine character, learning and growing from the most dreadful of experiences.

78

The majority of men spend their lives unconsciously immersed in a kind of debilitating habit, custom, or routine which offers them comfort and contentment while depriving them of the most essential elements of their lives. It would seem as if such a man were never born.

79

Technology, invention, and the entire modern enterprise have been designed to improve the external state of man, yet man continues to decay from within and has only a shrill, unsophisticated, childish, and boorish clown provided for his spiritual guidance.

80

It is common knowledge that what a man puts into his body in the form of food will affect his physical performance to a large degree. Yet, even possessed with this understanding, man remains notoriously unfit and sickly. He is similarly aware that exposing one's soul to the equivalent of intellectual or cultural junk food will have a comparable effect on the spirit as poor nutrition has on the body. Yet, he bides his time within a cultural wasteland of artistic bombast, superficiality, and titillation.

81

Woe be to the man who does not suffer for he has truly lost the key to character. The great man learns how to reap the benefits of his suffering and mold his character into something better. At any rate, a man should come to view the obstacles in his life as something of a gift since the great man is often he who perseveres. The more obstacles that one encounters, the more opportunity one possesses to show themselves to be a person of significance.

82

A man must surrender to those forces outside his control — willingly, slavishly — while simultaneously mounting an expedition to explore the perimeters of those very same limitations.

83

Human evolution includes a tendency for man to be a creature of the herd in order that he might maximize his own safety. Yet, in order to further evolve beyond the animal self, a man must learn to distrust this instinct.

84

In matters of the spirit, a man is rarely moved by argument and more readily prone to inspiration.

85

Rigidity in thought signifies a rigidity of character as well. Yet, for the spirit to be truly alive, it must be allowed to remain fluid. To force it into a mold merely petrifies it and makes of a man's character something waxen and lifeless.

86

The existentialist and the religious man each view consciousness as a kind of curse instead of as a gift that allows nature the opportunity to reflect upon herself. In fact, a man would never know himself at all if he were not first conscious of himself as distinct. For the religious man, the problem of consciousness is that it shakes him out of his strong inclination to return to the womb of oblivion since he finds his actual existence to be such a burden on him. The existentialist, on the other hand, is merely pointing out some of the particular problems related to consciousness itself. Awareness, for the great man, however, is always something that he wishes to see increased.

87

It is reason and logic which determine that the spirit does not exist, but one will never convince a man entirely of this fact because he *feels* it to be true. He may rename the spirit "mind" or "consciousness" or the like, but he's essentially speaking about the same thing. To utilize only the faculty of reason in determining the truth of the matter is to eliminate a whole slew of other perspectives, some of which could be quite illuminating. This is not to say that a man should eliminate reason entirely. To do so would be to make a similar mistake in trusting the conclusions of the intuition alone.

88

The value of a *well chosen* book exceeds the worth of a well chosen friend since the book will not engage in small talk or distraction of any kind. Instead, it will lead to the better development of a man's character than will the many banal diversions inherent in friendship.

89

The vast majority of men fight to the death for their external freedom — this facade of autonomy — yet keep themselves in chains from within.

90

Romantic love, if it is to be love, requires a passionate commitment, the same type of devotion as that which is required for the cultivation and development of a great man. Love, in fact, is the only means by which most men ever experience the depths of their own spirit and an inner connection with all of existence. They are able to inhabit the artistic perspective if but for a moment, much like the actual artist might — briefly. So, their understanding of passion and commitment in this sense is usually fleeting. They allow their passions to cool and, instead of finding new ways to reignite the flame, they abandon their faithfulness altogether, hoping to find it again with a different lover. This new love, of course, will require a similar commitment and the process begins anew. Or, they may remain steadfast to lovers who are unworthy of devotion, mistaking a desire to proliferate comfort and safety for passion.

12

The State of the Human Being

1

The difficulty with being the poet of one's own life, as Nietzsche would have it, and composing a life story so well assembled and unified that nothing could be subtracted without spoiling the whole, is that it is an impossible task. After all, so few men are artists and possess the kind of ability that such a project would demand. It is difficult enough to ask an artist to produce something great within his own medium, which contains elements that are much more malleable than the materials that make up the life of a man. I would dare say that no one has ever accomplished the task of making his life into a great work of art. Of course, there are revisionists that arrive upon the scene years after a man has passed who begin to weave a tale that make it *seem* as if their subject was just such a man, but these are mostly works of fiction..

2

Be prepared to abandon all common sense, you who would not be a commoner.

3

The good life, in fact the best life, is to live in accordance with one's own better nature.

4

There are a variety of proper ways to live one's life and the perspective which constitutes the "best" life will depend greatly upon the character of a man. The best life is, however, only marginally concerned with material goods beyond the acquisition of what is necessary for survival. The best wish to stuff their hearts and souls full of treasure while the worst are interested in little more than filling their coffers.

5

One only truly begins to enjoy the material goods of the world when he successfully learns to care little about acquiring them.

6

I make no pretense to argue or reason for what constitutes a good life. I can merely point the way for those who might wish to venture out to find their path. Christianity, that bastion of servility, is for those who have little inclination to engage themselves. They would prefer the work were done for them.

7

One's instinct should be properly humbled by one's reason and one's reason should be properly humbled by one's instinct. A certain amount of humility is a necessary characteristic of the higher man because he is all too aware of his own inadequacy.

8

A man delights in reason as he would any of his unique powers, yet it is nothing more than the strength of a lion or the speed of a gazelle. A condescending gazelle that looks down his nose at those who do not possess his speed seems a laughable thing indeed to the lion feasting on him.

9

Only if a man is willing to follow his deepest passions to their *logical* conclusion (which is not the same as success) will he live at peace with himself. Yet, he should not be blinded from the understanding that often our deepest passions will fade in their intensity over time and give way to surrounding fires that also need to be stoked and allowed to burn.

10

The *feeling* of justice precedes its reasoning.

11

Any book that doesn't read as if the genius sibling of your own mind is a waste of an afternoon and should be put away immediately for another time when you might be better suited. Never pick it up again if it reads as a dumber cousin.

12

At the very heart of philosophy — or at least should be at the heart — is the pondering of the question: "How shall I best live my life?"

13

An uneducated intuition is a blind boy without a cane.

14

The only evil that has ever been or will ever be can be attributed to the fanatic and his followers — religious, political, or otherwise. Learn moderation in all things if you wish to avoid such demons within yourself.

15

The goal of every man is to seek his imagined destiny and then be not afraid to follow it — especially since it rarely takes him to where he would have it lead. Yet, to do so, he must first develop and cultivate an ear for the song of fate and distinguish it from the warble of the Sirens.

16

The active reader seeks to understand and be understood. The passive reader hopes to kill a few hours of himself.

17

It is not a child's innocence that should be envied since that is more ignorance than anything else. Instead, one should emulate the passion of a child. The child is intimately connected to what moves him to action and animates his being. It is only the hindrance of the adult which might sway the child or force him to spend his time engaged in any other activity than that which fills his heart at the moment. This is not to say that one should live their life as would a child — there are too many pitfalls and stupidities inherent within such a view — but that one should instead find a way to reconnect the path of communication between one's heart and one's head that was severed during one's schooling.

18

Be wary not to suffer fools too gladly lest they make a fool of you as well.

19

Man is often mistaken about the project of his life. Typically he believes it to be an occupation of some sort. Yet, more often than not, it is his avocation that serves to define him. The farmer's project is not his crops. He tills to eat. What he does in the meantime will tell you more about his character.

20

A man will rarely thank you for belying his contentment, though it may be the greatest gift ever offered to him.

21

The danger of pathos is that a man will be tempted to feel without thinking. The danger of logos is that he will be tempted to think without feeling. A man should instead aim to develop his own ethos.

22

The overabundance of consciousness is one of the greatest blessings that can be bestowed upon a man though he views it as something of a curse, primarily because men have the greatest difficulty letting go of anything.

23

Suicide is the pessimistic expression of self-love.

24

Hope is a kind of amusement that man uses to distract himself from the reality that his situation is ultimately hopeless.

25

Man spends too much time extolling his virtues and little time at all developing and maintaining them.

26

Live your life in the manner that would best exemplify the greatness of this creature called "man."

27

Nothing of a man's accomplishments will bring him even a fraction as much enjoyment as that found in sitting by the seaside reflecting for hours about all that consciousness perceives — allowing any thought to overtake him at any given moment and putting aside the concerns of those responsibilities put upon him by others. Those that then record these musings for posterity are those that should be owed the debt of gratitude by subsequent generations who might model themselves in a similar manner. Society, of course, disparages such people as dreamers, shirkers and worse but only because most men have long ago shut their souls to the experience of life and secretly envy the man who has refused to accept an early death.

28

To argue with the fundamentalist is to argue with a child. He will never be convinced nor his perspective changed until he matures. It is a fruitless venture which should never be undertaken in the first place.

29

A great man does not disguise his vices with virtues, he transforms them into such.

30

Regret is inevitable except for those unconscious of themselves.

31

The search for character works in much the same manner as the fairy tale — a child is born of humble origin, discovers by chance that he is truly a prince, and then through many journeys, trials, and tribulations, proves himself to be what was proclaimed of him in the beginning. The majority of men, alas, remain satisfied with the discovery of their princely title and travel no farther along the way to demonstrate the validity of their royal claim.

32

In a godless universe that doubtless will one day cease to exist, the hedonist seems to have the most rational philosophy — enjoy as many pleasures as possible since pleasure appears to be the only good. Yet, even pleasure has its division into ranks. There are pleasures of the body and those of the spirit — physical and ephemeral. The spiritual pleasures outrank pleasures of the body because they are more satisfactory to the man. However, the child much prefers the bodily pleasures since they are the only ones to which he has access. Spiritual pleasures of contemplation require considerable cultivation in order to be enjoyed, so they are available only to someone predisposed and committed to experiencing them. Such spirits are rewarded for their labors by the delight of languishing in the sublime pleasure of contemplation for its own sake.

33

To focus on anything other than what can be construed as the most important elements of your existence is to mistake the sun for the moon and waste the day sleeping.

34

How wistfully and full of envy does man watch the caged tiger lolling listlessly among the foliage of his enclosure. "What a great life," man exclaims "free from the constraints of the wild." The tiger is living well, he believes, because this is the average man's ideal — safely caged, pampered, and admired. He will gladly abandon the passions of his soul for such a life since they merely serve to frighten him anyway. He is quite content to make all that is great into mediocrity.

35

Love is more of an idea than it is a feeling. However, man does possess grand feelings for great ideas.

36

The negation of the will, the movement toward will-less-ness of the Buddhist, is quite simply a will to suicide. One must instead cultivate the will and teach it to desire things more worthy than merely pleasure and satiation.

37

The difference between a man with wisdom and one without is the amount of consciousness and conscience with which he experiences his world.

38

There are a great many helpful rules that when followed dutifully can enable a man to live a long and productive life. They should not be confused, however, for principles that will enhance the quality or significance of a man's life. In fact, they may even hinder that purpose to a large extent.

39

As Nietzsche suggests, a man should hold a deep affection for the unfolding of his fate provided that he has chosen it for himself. This is not to imply that a man has control over the ultimate outcome of his fate, so many elements of fortune having been given to him at the outset. Yet, the fact that he has willfully chosen to embark upon the journey of finding what is truly genuine and authentic to his providence, at the expense oftentimes of worldly success, will fill him with a feeling of satisfaction with his overall destiny, warts and all. The greater mass of men will never feel such a thing, driven as they are in forcing their wishes upon the external world.

40

If it is true that the will of man is comprised of the "will to power" which then leads him to dominate or subjugate anyone or anything in his way as a means of acquiring this power again and again, then it is true only of man's animal nature — consequently relegating him to something lower than a beast who does not possess such a trait. The industrial age has certainly made a case for the existence of such a power with its overabundance of manmade genocide, war, tyranny, and fanatic fundamentalism. Yet, there can be a more cultivated and refined expression of such a power if it be used as an animating force to a higher principle, if a man were to sublimate his thirst for domination with a desire to instead create.

41

A man does not simply feel his emotions, Sartre explained, as if overtaken by some great and powerful wave; he chooses them in so far as they reflect the particular disposition with which he has decided to face the situation. In this manner, a man can sometimes look to his emotions for guidance.

42

There are two kinds of suffering in the world, that which is inflicted by nature and that which is inflicted by man. The former are inevitable to a large degree while the latter need not exist at all if it were not that man is such a repugnant creature generally. Yet, both of these conditions of suffering are to some extent unavoidable. Mankind will never rid itself of its evil characters anymore than nature will rid itself of insects. Therefore, the good man should prepare himself to meet both of these prospects in abundance so that he might not succumb to either.

43

The sufferings that arise from nature are without malice or intent and are, to a certain extent, inescapable. While it may be possible to prevent or forestall certain natural sufferings, others will eventually take their place to demonstrate that suffering is something that is unavoidable and perhaps even inherently necessary at times. So a man must prepare himself for this eventuality since mostly through suffering will he develop and cultivate his character. Any fool can seem noble and fine during the untroubled periods of his life, but it takes a true man of character to arise graciously and upright from a bout with misery. The man who complains of suffering, like a child, rejects the notion that the world is constructed so and beats his breast for the creation of a better universe. Yet, none will arise except in the multicolored space of his imagination. So, he will either choose some form of suicide or he will show himself to be a higher man of dignity.

44

A man must include idleness within his day if he wishes to live a good life. Idleness is different than distraction in that it seeks to avoid nothing but is actively engaged, even passionately so, with the present moment — awash in contemplation and appreciation of the world around — loafing, as Whitman calls it, and taking pleasure through the soul in the simple joy of life itself.

45

A man should be careful, however, not to become lost in idleness. It is too easy to accept idleness as a kind of philosophy; the beautiful song of the siren makes the listener wish to live forever entranced by the tune. Yet, this, too, can lead to a kind of suicide. To make a life of pure idleness is to commit oneself to tedium ultimately and the dreary prospect of becoming nothing at all — a dull acorn that refuses the call of the oak.

46

One of the great qualities to be found in a man is his righteous perseverance in the face of overwhelming opposition. One of the basest qualities of a man is his stubbornness in the face of overwhelming evidence that he might be wrong.

47

Loyalty is only a virtue if its object is worthy of the allegiance. How pitiful is the dog who remains true to an unworthy master?

48

The man who places barely any value on possessions will give little care as to whether he actually possesses them or not. Thus, he will be freed from the concerns of the vast majority of men who labor, steal and war to acquire and keep material goods — an activity that dominates the bulk of man's waking hours and holds him as a kind of slave of his own perspective.

49

Everyone in their turn, if they have children, spends time as a supreme ruler, either king or queen, and receives a glimpse into how they would fare as sovereign to the world. Some prove themselves to be tyrants, others are weak and ineffectual, some are beggars, some are thieves, some show themselves to be wildly popular while ultimately leading their subjects to ruin, and still others may be unjust but kindly. The disasters that they make of their brief rule are mitigated by the fact that they have so few citizens under their watch and care. And this is true, of course, except when one thinks of all the unsuitable sovereigns that populate the world and how dreadfully they govern their realm. What began as a private reign multiplies to become a public tyranny. Since they rule their children this way, it is likely they rule themselves in just such a manner and the problem compounds itself again. The higher man is he who rules himself and others with wisdom, fairness, moderation, efficiency, and a patient disposition.

50

A man does not construct his character as much as he discovers it, the creative act being the cultivation of certain found elements that he wishes to accentuate and further develop while keeping rein upon those which he perceives to be of lesser value. He is engaged in the process of carving out the statue from the rock.

51

Concern with being "true" to one's character or "true" to oneself is to overvalue the element of consistency demanded by those "hobgoblins of little minds."

52

While wisdom is available to be had by all, invariably, only a few attain it. For only these few are eager to make the necessary sacrifice

53

Love is both a virtue and a vice, depending upon how it is used and cultivated. The man who loves the wrong things, for instance, possesses love as a vice. He has fixed his passion on something unworthy and must now focus it elsewhere if he is to become a better man. Yet, if he truly loves such a thing he will find it extremely difficult, if not impossible, to divorce it from his heart. A man might also possess the vice of loving too much so that he does not attend to other important elements of his existence. Or he might love possessively so that he begins to hoard the thing he loves. It is only if he loves the right things at the right times and in the appropriate ways, as Aristotle suggests, that love is something of a virtue. For this, of course, he will need to cultivate a good intuition and exercise more than a little self-control.

54

The possession of any or all of the virtues that have been historically significant to man does not necessarily equate to happiness nor may a man inevitably believe that his life was well lived on account of his possession of them, prone as he is to thinking of happiness and contentment to be qualities that will fill him with enduring and changeless satisfaction. Rather, the well-lived life is a judgment based on the character of a man and his accomplishments compared to those who came before him. For this higher conception of the good life a man will be in need of virtue since a depraved man will not compare favorably to the great men of the past and a man whose actions or achievements are shallow, insincere, or downright immoral indeed will find that he does not bear good comparison either. For the lower man, however, a well-lived life merely consists in the accumulation of as many pleasures, possessions, and experiences as he can muster in the span of his short and not particularly admirable existence.

55

Jealousy arises because of a man's misguided notion of ownership. It is an arrogant rejection of fate and an egotistical perception of what he believes he is due. Until a man comes to the mature realization that he deserves absolutely nothing in this world and is due not even his next breath, he will always be forced to confront the multi-headed beast of envy.

56

Man everywhere finds himself in situations which he neither chose nor has any control to alter. Yet, he does have a say as to how he shall face his unfortunate, as well as fortunate, circumstances. If he is to find himself a prisoner to his occupation, will he remain cordial and refined, still aspiring to a kind of personal excellence or will he wail and lament his fate, making life even more unpleasant for himself and others? If he finds himself a giant of industry, rich and powerful beyond his wildest dreams, will he flaunt his wealth and abuse his authority or will he be generous and kind, making sure that he uses his influence for benefits that include the world entire? These are issues of character and are more significant to a man's life than the fated accidents that might befall him.

57

A man should be careful, however, to distinguish those elements of his life which are fated and beyond his control from those which spring from the nature of his delusions and ignorance. This is a difficult task since a man is often unaware of his own lack of perception, depth, and understanding. He will need to make a habit of being brutally honest with himself and develop a certain humility with respect to what he holds as true.

58

There is no doctrine which might show what is absolutely true, right, good, or beautiful for all men at all times. Theory and doctrine only demonstrate these qualities to particular men at particular times — the common men who derive comfort from the notion of a universally rational and law governed universe. Science would hope to champion a doctrine or law such as that which regulates the path of the sun for the heart of man, but human nature does not innately conform to the rational. Instead, reason is merely one of the means by which a man aspires to improve himself. Yet, as with all of the virtues, it must be used wisely — in moderation.

59

The creative side of man is his higher self in action. He transforms the brute reality of existence to express a value that is not found in nature itself — these are the virtues and the manifold works of art that are antithetical to the striving for food, shelter, possessions, and Darwinian procreation.

60

The present only possesses meaning and significance in the act of contemplating and reflecting on it. Living in the here and now requires contemplation and one only truly exists in such a state to the extent that he is reflective. Thus, the appreciation of life, the realization of profundity

205

in experience, and the perception of transcendence are only understood when a man extricates himself from the hurly-burly of everyday, common concerns and reflects on them. The poet's plea that man must live in the now and experience the present moment is really a demand that he cease understanding living as an action and perceive it more as something of an important thought.

61

Confrontation with the great, vast, eternal nothingness of the universe — the determined and unrelenting wrestling with the abyss — is a necessary element for the cultivation of character. In fact, such an action often sets the whole process into motion.

62

Many people wish that their life was similar to a movie or a play. What they desire aren't necessarily the adventures or experiences of those upon the stage or screen, but the elimination of all the mundane, banal, and insignificant moments of their lives so that what is revealed are only those essential moments of substance. Yet, they will of course recoil at the resulting length of their life and wish that they had spent their time more wisely.

63

The more a man attempts to better his external circumstances, the less he will attend to the betterment of his spirit and so he might come to amass all the riches of the world and still find that he possesses nothing of much value — that is, if he is blessed with any insight at all. Most will simply suffocate beneath their material treasures, blissfully unaware of any other view but the one perceived from this vantage point.

64

A man truly owns nothing — not his spouse, his children, his friends, his possessions, his property or even himself. Yet, modern man is thrown into a circumstance where he is afforded the opportunity to avail himself of a plethora of riches, more or less. The dichotomy of this situation is that he cannot simply dismiss these goods as something altogether meaningless or else he will suffer from the poverty of existence, surrendering everything to Caesar and starving in the process. Yet, he must not hoard these treasures either lest he break his neck beneath their weight.

65

Beneath the veneer of character lies a vast sea of uncharted desires, motivations, temperaments, drives, and regrets. A man is born with a certain temperament or disposition, but without character of any kind. His character only arises when he begins to make choices for his life. Every choice, of course, is enacted from a confluence of events, circumstances, unconscious elements, and temperaments, as if the multiplicity of selves within a man were collaboratively working to create the work of art that is his character.

66

Men spend the bulk of their days in a sound slumber, sleepwalking their way through the vast majority of their lives. Though they may hear the alarms to rouse them from this state of existence, by and large they merely choose to ignore them.

67

The Aristotelian final end, that ultimate goal for the sake of which there exists no further aim, is different for each man according to his talents and character. The lower man may find pleasure or wealth to be his final goal and will live quite content to exist in such a manner, whereas the great man would find such an aim to be entirely unsatisfying and beneath him, which, of course, it would be. Humanity, as a whole, however, does not share in any one particular final end between them.

68

A man who is not inclined, either by talent or desire, toward deep reflection cannot be convinced that his life would be richer with the possession of it any more than the deaf man can imagine a better life with music in it. Those whose ears hear perfectly pity the deaf for this one missing element, the spiritual and emotional richness that music brings. Likewise, the man who spends his spare time in quiet contemplation and often bittersweet, melancholy reflection, pities the rest of mankind for its lack of awareness.

69

It is far too easy to immerse oneself in the hurly-burly of everyday experience and spend few, if any, moments in quiet reflection, pondering the significance of it all. So, like a man caught in a riptide and carried out to sea for 60 years only to be dumped upon the shore at the moment of his death, an entire life is spent in fruitless labor, striving merely against the current of experience.

70

The Romans used biography as a means of instructing others to excellence through the example of an excellent soul. The modern man, on the other hand, utilizes biography as a means to better understand how to improve his external circumstance.

71

For the most part, the true hero remains obscured from the gaze of the multitude since he seeks no reward greater than the possession of his character and his virtue.

72

Only through an honest and *committed* struggle to seek the fate that you desire will you ever discover the fate that is your portion. The rest will tacitly accept a destiny that is beneath them.

73

A man must cultivate the need to have few needs except for those necessities which might enliven his spirit. In fact, he should cultivate the desire for only these needs and little else besides — except, of course, for what nature demands of him.

74

In order to hear the voice within and make of it his own, a man must first learn to tune his ear to it. This requires a kind of willful disregard for the other possibilities of a man's existence, at least until one can discern the message of one's better nature.

75

The only thing that a man can truly know for certain is that which resides within his own heart — and even that will be a fleeting insight.

76

A man will sometimes start to believe that he is not free because he is not afforded choices that he *desires* to possess. Yet, as Sartre points out, a man is still free to choose within the limitations of his specific situation. If nothing else he possesses the freedom to choose to refuse. He also decides the attitude with which he intends to confront his condition.

13

The State of the Higher Man

1

The true Elites, those who are deserving of both the name and its responsibilities, are those souls who, as the name suggests, distinguish themselves as being "higher" than the common stock of mankind. However, this is not to be determined by one's accomplishments or social status, let alone the accumulation of material possessions, but as a determination of one's character. Further, the determination of a man's character cannot be sufficiently decided until after his death, when all of the evidence presents itself. Thus, the living can only *aspire* to being among the class of the elites. Those who aspire to more common aims — money, status, power, notoriety, pleasure, contentment, etc. — will, no doubt, achieve their aims and be appropriately ranked among the commoners.

2

It has been the fashion of late to try to establish the commoner as some kind of heroic beast who fights to achieve his freedom from the political elites. However, this is an entirely different class of elites than the one that I wish to discuss. The political and cultural elites are, more often than not, simply commoners dressed in kingly robes, deluding themselves with the belief that the possession of knowledge, power, taste, wealth, or fame provides them with some sort of special privilege, conveniently forgetting the significant role that chance has played in their acquisition of each.

3

There must be a new interpretation of humanity; a positive definition of elitism where the limitations of individualism leave off; an incorporation of the individual into the larger society through excellence that dispenses with egotism.

4

The cult of the "common man" has transformed from a movement to liberate mankind from the restraints of unjustified nobility to a celebration of that which is ignoble.

5

The French have a term, *Noblesse Oblige*, which roughly means that whoever claims to be a noble must likewise conduct himself nobly. Similarly, all men, if they are to substantiate their claim to be something more than the lowliest and cruelest of the animals, must live up to the responsibilities that such a lofty stature demands. How many few among you can honestly meet such a prerequisite? Yet, how many claim a right to wear the crown nonetheless?

6

Mankind has reduced Nietzsche's idea of the superman to a comic book hero because the character seems much less complex in that form. So far has man strayed from the original meaning and yet so closely does he resemble the cartoonish facade.

7

The higher man finds no satisfaction with complacency — however tempting might be the thought. His bliss belongs, by definition, to the labors of his heart. He is a seeker primarily who is duty bound to endure the worst for the sake of cultivating his spirit. He will stand to every torture laid before him — every hardship — that he might learn and make something greater of himself — perhaps even divine. It is a task which just might require a lifetime to perfect, yet he is prepared for it. These are the exemplars of humankind who find it quite absurd to laze about eternity in splendor — reminiscing; content; and dispassionate to a fault.

8

The distinction of the higher man is merely an honorary title. It has nothing to do with fame and everything to do with character and the overall aim of his life. The moment a man perceives himself to be such a creature and begins to act as if it bestowed on him some special privilege, he immediately proves otherwise.

9

It is the individuals who courageously wrestle with death, loss, alienation, anxiety, despair, guilt, fear, and dread, but forge onward to find meaning in spite of these afflictions, that most exemplify the higher man. He does not seek refuge from these realities by suicide, distraction, or delusion. He is the doomed soldier who does not abandon the fight even with the awareness that he will ultimately lose.

10

Wisdom should be one of the desired goals of the higher man. It is not attained by reason or spirit alone but by a confluence of these attributes through study and experience.

11

Wisdom is the final realization of the interconnectedness of all things — the artist's perspective.

12

The synthesis of the forces within is the proper state to which the higher man aspires — moderation, balance, and proportion.

13

In the sense that I am an artist, I'm a philosopher. In the sense that I am a philosopher, I'm an artist.

14

All anti-intellectual sentiments arise from a bitterness in those who feel incapable of the enjoyment of intellectual pursuits. The insecurity that is inherent in such an individual manifests itself through a deep rooted hatred of the intellect. The story of Aesop in which the fox rejects his desire for the grapes that he can't attain is illustrative of this idea. Yet, this is not to say that such an individual is completely unable to attain such pleasures if he puts a concerted effort toward doing so, but it is perhaps more difficult for him because of his natural capacities. His anti-intellectualism then results from a kind of surrender in the face of a difficult challenge — that and his egotistical disdain for feeling inferior to anything.

15

The wise man tolerates the dogmatist in the same manner in which the parent tolerates the child — with a sense of amusement until there are important matters to decide. With respect to such matters of significance, the parent simply ignores the input of the child and if the child becomes too indignant about this treatment, the parent will banish him from the conversation altogether.

16

I provide no reasons for my opinions here, not because none went into the formation of them, but because I have no desire to persuade others of my beliefs. The righteous need prove nothing by their words but by their deeds alone. So act!

17

The higher man is well aware that all shall fade away from existence — fame, power, wealth, love, art, man, animal. Given enough time everything will be swept into the yawning chasm of nothingness and oblivion. He knows that his labor is ultimately futile, yet he labors on regardless of this fact. The common man, meanwhile, busies himself with distractions.

18

The truly superior man will treat even the town idiot graciously for he feels little need to display his excellence as a trophy. He simply *is* excellent — as demonstrated by his gracious treatment of the fool.

19

The higher man will display deference to all and allegiance to none.

20

A man with a great spirit has learned to view the world entirely in shades of different hues, some more brilliant than others, yet all somehow blend and color the richness of the world.

21

To be well read will often pass as wise to those who read little or not at all.

22

The great man is rarely able and never desires to forget himself entirely.

23

Man is not only a relation of the chimpanzee but quite often he proves himself to be in closer relation to him than to the higher man.

24

The will to power is a masculine trait whose ultimate byproduct is the warrior, the tyrant, and the bully. The will to cultivate (also a power of sorts) is a feminine trait whose byproducts are culture, wisdom, and the artist.

25

Consciousness strips man of all excuses for his bestial manner and demands his responsibility as something higher.

26

Man likes to believe that greatness springs from the womb as a kind of gift bestowed upon the world by the gods. In so doing, he obscures the fact that greatness only arises as a kind of passion initially, a desire to question and to understand. Great men have only a passing desire for any of the other, more superficial, benefits of life — fame, power, pleasure, wealth, friendship, etc.. The man of mediocrity would rather believe in greatness as a divine blessing to absolve himself of the sacrifice and diligence that would be required of him as well if he were to undertake the task. He would rather curse the fates than recognize his own laziness.

27

"He who dies with the most money, wins," sayeth the materialist. "He who dies with fame, wins," sayeth the man of reputation. "He who dies with God, wins," sayeth the village idiot. "He who dies with the most friends, wins," sayeth the optimist. "Nobody wins," sayeth the pessimist. "Oh, you children and your silly games," sighs the wise man.

28

The great man has no desire to parent the multitude of children that go by the name of "man." His concern is primarily internal and his project is to better his understanding of the cosmos and himself within it. Occasionally this leads to the benefit of all humanity, but it is merely of secondary concern.

29

Can there be a modern equivalent to the "gentleman" of the Renaissance or the "genius" of the later period — something to which all men may aspire? The Cosmopolitan, perhaps? The Mensch?

30

Man barely pierces the surface of his own depth when, out of social dogma or sentimental yearnings, he marries young and brings another life into the world — thus producing three incomplete beings. At the consummation of such a marriage a man typically begins to forget (if he ever knew) that he might be destined for something greater. Once his child is born the probability that he will ever suspect himself capable of anything greater than raising it becomes unlikely. Only the child might then break the cycle, providing he disobeys his parent's desire that he, too, should marry young and propagate.

31

The wise man is ever a fool to the fool himself.

32

Keep friends with only the greatest of men though it mean you possess no friend who is currently alive.

33

To cultivate the better elements of one's nature is the only truly worthwhile task of man. The rest of his undertakings merely adorn his name, which is itself a meaningless trinket that was stamped upon him from without.

34

A man should spend the greater amount of his energies upon those projects that extend beyond the measure of his short little life. All other projects are petty.

35

If it makes no difference what you do, say, feel, or think; if all the world is essentially meaningless and your contribution just as empty as anyone else's; if it is not significant one way or the other whether you be a murderer, saint, liar, or cheat, yet, still you choose the path of good character; that, my friend, is a true man.

36

Of course Emerson believed that he could look inward and find the well spring of profundity and strength. He was a great spirit after all. The average man, on the other hand, finds merely a muddy puddle.

37

The only way to truly influence the child is to inspire him by one's example. This is also the means by which the great spirits may sway the lesser.

38

Self-fulfillment to the common man is nothing more than self-content and self-content, at least in any extended state, is anathema to the man of higher spirit.

39

The wise man knows to eliminate desire and cultivate his passion instead.

40

Consistency of thought often betrays shallowness in one's thinking.

41

The humanity of man is not to be found in his weaknesses, as the religious might have you believe, but in his creativity to surpass those weaknesses of character and transform them into strengths.

42

The triumph of the human spirit, it is believed, is to endure while maintaining a positive perspective of the world. Yet, any animal can endure in such a manner. Consciousness is the problem here for man, so man needs his little lies in order to sustain himself. Job endures while maintaining his trust in God. However, it is precisely this trust that allows him to endure — take it from him and he would become like an orphaned child, mewling for guidance and heartsick for the return of his daddy. Thus Job is no example of the exultant spirit of man. Job would need to wholeheartedly accept that his situation was without reason — its meaning no more than what he honestly found in it — and that oblivion awaited him when his sufferings were complete. If he then smiled and laughed at his festering sores and used the experience to discover something of himself and wrote poetry about the beauty of the world, the sublimity of experience, then could he be celebrated as a model man.

43

The great man has only the greatest souls from ages past to befriend him. For this reason does he spend so much of his time in books. In contrast, his contemporaries, other than those few rare exceptions who probability suggests he will never meet, are a dull and uninspiring lot.

44

One should not suffer fools gladly, but lightly nonetheless.

45

The higher man is an explorer more than he is a conqueror since nothing that he finds can be truly claimed as his own. It belongs to all of humanity and will be once again returned to them upon his death. The truest joy of life for man is the exploration of the infinite abyss

46

A man must be willing to abandon all ideologies, even those closest to him, if he wishes to lift his spirit above the commoner.

47

All men great and small must necessarily sacrifice their own self-interest from time to time to others, presumably for the greater good. The great man will eventually learn to recognize the greater part of himself and refuse to sacrifice it for something lesser.

48

The reason that the higher men are so few in number is that it requires a spirit made of air to be able to accept the truths of existence in all their terrible honesty. His is a melancholy perspective that is often dismissed as pessimistic and thereby unfruitful and too terrifying to accept without a few "harmless lies" designed to make a man less likely to fall into utter despair and suicide. Most men lack the strength of character to forge ahead despite the loss of those universal truths that have sustained the common man for centuries.

49

The great man searches, the common man concedes.

50

The common man finds his self-worth at the expense of others in competition. The higher man competes only with himself and finds his worth in transcending himself.

51

The higher man is not necessarily the man of any particular accomplishment or status since such things are at the mercy of fate. Instead, he is the personage of restraint, virtue, and wisdom. His accomplishment can be found in his character and his fate has no bearing upon it.

52

The man of genius is he who can introduce some new moral sentiment to the human understanding, or inspire a different manner of thinking or feeling about the universe. His is the fire that ignites the consciousness of man to burn in some new direction. Yet, even these ideas will one day become the machinery of the status quo and need to be overcome.

53

The man of genius exists in a higher state of being than the common man, more perceptive, sensitive, and attuned to the world around him. Consequently, there is no place for him in the modern industrial age – the era of indifference. He is the shaman and the sage of previous generations, the man of visions. Yet, to an age that worships only material things, he is seen as something of a crank.

54

Spend not one moment of your life in envy of those poor souls who flit about the earth engaged in an unending volley of experiences, swept along by the rushing tide of spectacle and performance, enveloped by admirers and critics alike who all demand attention and sacrificial tidings, consumed by the striving for immortal accomplishment to pad their hardened graves. They have squandered the only thing that possesses ultimate value for the higher man — contemplation and reflection.

55

A man can only be great to the extent that he recognizes and celebrates his own limited animal nature as well as the gifts of consciousness that allow him to contemplate the cosmos. He must accept that his greatness isn't his own but something that he shares with the great spirits of antiquity and exists for him only momentarily.

56

The only thing that a man has the capacity to control is his attitude toward the outcomes of his life that fate has decided for him. In this manner he has the ability to control, not his destiny, but his bearing in relation to it. This is how we might find an unhappy man with an outrageously fortunate destiny and a happy man with a miserable one. The latter's life seems more desirable but it is in contrast to the external circumstances that one would expect a man to envy. It is the development of character that molds a man's attitudes towards his fate and makes him grateful for everything that comes his way. It is the wisdom of character that helps him moderate his desires and experiences so that he might not turn a virtue into a sin.

57

Anything that fails to better prevails to ruin.

58

When you tame the "savage beast," he always seems the duller for it. Look at his eyes afterward, listless and uncaring, slow, sleepy and lethargic. He has been forced to submit and submission for a spirited creature is a kind of death for him too.

59

In order to stave off the ill effects of boredom, primarily the desire for distraction and unworthy diversion, one must pursue a passionate desire that can at once be satisfied without being purged — a lifelong project that is in some sense creative. Yet, it must lead to a better understanding of the inner man as well.

60

Suffering itself will lead ultimately to either more suffering and eventually to despair or suicide (distraction) or it can serve as a tool to discover and cultivate those passions which cannot be ultimately extinguished except by death. In this manner suffering has meaning if a man perceives it for this end.

61

The man of the industrial age is not afflicted much by the sufferings of need for he has now satisfied these basic elements for himself many times over. Seldom does he find himself desiring basic needs for which he cannot somewhat quickly satisfy. He does, however, suffer from the torments of boredom and these trouble him to such an extent that he welcomes the sufferings of primitive man as a means to overcome the monotony of his life. His religion now, too, has become merely a diversion for him. He is a suicide who still walks the earth unaware that he leapt to his death long ago.

62

It is the lower rank of men who commit what Camus refers to as "philosophical suicide." They accept conclusions and theories about life because it gives them definitive answers to questions that are either unanswerable or answered only with increasing complexity. They cannot live with the anxiety that arises from the confrontation with such inquiries because they lack the necessary courage to do so. The higher man, on the other hand, is one who is unafraid to venture out beyond the limits of the well defined, to seek and find whatever lies outside the city gates in the dark woods of the unknown. He may bring back boons to his community which might then modify their accepted conclusions in some fashion, yet the best that he can hope to bestow upon them is to awaken them from their slumber and inspire them to venture out themselves in search of what he has found — a unique, authentic self.

63

The higher man will always accept less than what is his share, not because he feels undeserving comparatively, but because the virtue of fairness is more important to him than whatever is being distributed into portions.

64

Great kings will so quickly fall once led by laws that might serve to raise some other creature.

65

The lower man should be pitied, not reviled. He has missed his only chance at consciousness, reflection, and understanding in this his only life. Instead, he exchanges these higher qualities for titillation, spectacle, distraction, and contentment at any cost. His actions, which inadvertently sully what is truly sacred and mutilate what is truly divine are, of course, despicable and he can certainly be held to blame more than can the morally unconscious animal, but he is too immature to be held in too much contempt. He, too, is somewhat morally unconscious, though not entirely unaccountable. His is the nature that befouls the name of man and makes him seem as if he were something of a beast. The task of the higher man then is to recover mankind's reputation.

66

The higher man rarely loses the feeling that all of creation is somehow divine and sacred, but these feelings arise because of his particular relation to the world, not because he senses the presence of some divine creator.

67

The higher man is an alchemist of sorts in that he turns even the most dreadful or common elements of experience into gold. He does not merely look on the bright side and ignore or forget all the rest, but incorporates his entire existence into the betterment of his character. He is never, then, a victim of his circumstance, or of anything else for that matter. A victim is, in relation to his assailant, the weaker soul. Yet, the higher man makes of his enemy a friend by utilizing the wrongs done against him to further strengthen and refine his spirit.

68

Imagine yourself a prisoner for life in a small cell with barely any window. The majority of men would spend their days attempting to forget the bleakness of their situation. They would immerse themselves in distracting labors of some sort, or medicate themselves, or even find the comfort of religion — anything to put their plight out of mind. Their life, for all intents and purposes, is over and they are merely killing time — the cowardly suicide. For William James and other pragmatists, such distractions would be useful and, therefore, acceptable ways to encounter the pains of existence. Yet, they are hardly commendable, as practical and understandable as they may be. The higher man, though he be a prisoner, would use the time to his advantage and examine his character through the light of this new situation. After all, the fate of a prisoner has certain similarities to the fate of a free man — both possess the limitation that little is within their control besides the content of their character and their attitude towards circumstances. A man in jail possesses the same opportunity to examine and cultivate his spirit. He might then begin to address certain questions. Is his soul merely the product of a privileged existence that cannot stand to the trials of adversity? Does his character have strength enough to withstand the horrors of true hopelessness and still remain virtuous? Will he conform to the misery of the place and allow himself to become overwhelmed with a few seemingly harmless distractions? Will he forget the spiritual project altogether and simply kneel before the God of organized religion?

69

It is perhaps more difficult for a king to forgo the temptations of his circumstance since it appears to him that he has no limitations at all. There is no hopelessness to his existence, or so it seems, and he feels that he may do whatever he pleases. While the prisoner can be led astray by the hopelessness of his situation, the king will become lost in the sheer distraction of possibility. He has no need of distraction to make him forget his misery. He is instead miserable by his distractions. They consume him and he is unable to find his way back to himself.

70

The higher man must look for avenues in which to test his merit since it is not a thing externally made manifest except through tribulation. Ordinary men venture out to test themselves in war, but the man of substance will refuse brute violence as a means by which to prove himself. With just such a refusal, in fact, contrary to the mongering of the mob, might he find his own battleground. Yet, he need not rely on such dramatic means when simple righteous endurance may suffice. The artist, for example, who labors for years in obscurity, tending to his art, may serve as an excellent model.

71

To be a great man, one must first choose great men to imitate. After all, no child ever learned to walk by watching his own two feet.

72

The higher man is not necessarily a position of worldly status, being more of a responsibility than a tribute of any kind. It is participation within the greatness of mankind that has existed for centuries — a lifting of oneself above the animal, not as a means for domination or boastfulness, but as a positioning of oneself where a man should rightfully belong were he not such an ignorant brute.

The higher man must be engaged in some kind of creative project that remains with him for the entirety of his life. As Nietzsche suggests, this should be the creation of one's own self. However, the cultivation of a man's character is usually accomplished by engaging in other projects that ultimately lead to this end. After all, the "creation of a self" is far too vague a notion to be able to know how it should be undertaken. Furthermore, it consists in something more substantial than merely looking within and acting on the feelings and desires that one discovers there. Therefore, a man must first choose some viable and fitting work to throw himself into, endeavors that are less abstract and esoteric, if he expects to accomplish the goal. Of course, every man is engaged in some kind of work, even those common fools who so greatly populate the earth. The man of character, however, will quickly dispense with any activity that does not suit the desired objective of beatifying or illuminating his own spirit and, by extension, the world around him, which is more than simply becoming who he is, but, more importantly, becoming who he ought to be within the world in which he finds himself. The common man becomes lost in a myriad of other distractions — health, wealth, progeny, reputation, power, illusion and amusement being the most customary forms. The overall project then is supported or undone by a host of smaller and more practical undertakings, some more significant or beneficial than others. Yet, a man should be cautioned not to mistake the forest for the trees. This is the problem that is often encountered by the artist and why their character is so frequently underdeveloped even while their work is so exceptional.

74

The higher man must try to become honest with himself. Men are, in general, easily fooled, especially by themselves, and they are too quick to accept the judgment of others as their own. They also lie to avoid certain uncomfortable truths about their character that they would rather believe otherwise. These qualities lead them ultimately along a path that is detrimental to their spirit. They become either some form of a narcissistic megalomaniac or a shriveled and fragile flower that cannot stand the light of day. So prevalent and pervasive is this tendency in man to spew falsehoods to himself that it is virtually impossible to eliminate altogether, but the higher man must remain vigilant in his attempts to try and purge it from his mind, remaining humbled and proud all at the same time. All men are often far better than they take themselves to be and far worse than they might imagine.

75

It is essential that the higher man be well read. He cannot possibly encounter all that the world has to offer through his everyday experience. Yet, he can multiply his exposure to the world through the written thoughts of other men whose ideas and existence are different than his own. This is truly better than even a face to face encounter with such a man because one seldom is afforded the opportunity to delve into the depths of a man's understanding and experience simply through conversation. Even if such a thing were commonplace, it would be impossible to do with those great men who have long since passed and from whom one often learns the most. Only through the written word is this accomplished. The greater the work, the more a man will benefit himself because of it.

76

The higher man must try to develop an artistic perspective of the world. The artist perceives the universe as something linked to all of existence, informing the nature of every man, tree, and bird. He recognizes the eternal nature of every passing moment and the true significance of death. For him, the world *is* poetry, even in its suffering. Yet, he does not achieve this through some established dogma, but by a heightened sensitivity to the world around him and an understanding of the symbolic nature of the universe. He is moral to his very core, in his heart at least, if not always in his actions, and he abhors those unmerciful and short-sighted fools whose vision is significantly myopic. Yet, he is aware that even they have a role to play since duality is something unified to him. He is awash in the mysteries of the universe and sees the absolute beauty of life, despite its misery, its torment, and its pain. In fact, these unfortunate qualities help to sweeten his attachment to the more appealing facets of existence. His is the perception of man at his most heightened state of awareness — that which small children often perceive instinctively — and it may be achieved again — one's daily grind having dulled it to a degree — by truly encountering the greatest works of man.

77

Patience is also something essential to the higher man as he will, no doubt, suffer a great many fools who will surround him in his daily life. Their stupidities will unnerve him and their wanton wastefulness of life and the world around them will make him wish to purge them from the earth. Yet, he must endure their ignorance and their fascination with banality if he is to remain as something more admirable than they. He must accept that his kind will never populate the earth to the same degree as the common fool and so he is to be forever outnumbered. However, this should be viewed as something of a gift. He has been spared the kind of existence that nature most abhors in men and has been given, instead, a touch of the divine. He will need patience to cultivate it because understanding does not immediately arrive upon the point of a lightening bolt and a garden does not bloom magically overnight.

78

Additionally, the higher man must be well-mannered and kind. There is little that betrays an immature soul like the display of rudeness or cruelty to others. It displays a weakness in character in that such actions are attempts to exhibit power or exert control, neither of which are attributes of a cultivated character and if, instead, it is the demonstration of a lack of control in oneself, then that, too, suggests a man who has yet to become a master of himself. The higher man has refined his emotions and civilized his soul to such an extent that he understands rudeness as the wildness of a child and cruelty as the viciousness of the human animal, neither of whom belong in a civilized society. These are common qualities of a man, especially an immature one, but the higher man is he whose stature is precisely above the common herd. While manners are an artificial and arbitrary custom, the higher man, unlike the childish soul, recognizes their value for bringing cohesion and civilization to the world, thus making it a place more orderly and meaningful in which to live. Kindness, too, is logically deduced to be something which any man would admit a desire to have it returned to him in kind. Tipping his cap with a kindly "good morning" does not make him submissive and weak, but rather exemplifies the vitality and strength of his character. He is so fortified from within that authenticity exudes from him even when engaged in practices that might seem otherwise false and superficial.

79

The higher man is likewise passionate, but this differs from simply being awash in feeling as any child might be. All emotion must be cultivated to a certain degree so that its expression is a controlled, measured, and proper response appropriate to the circumstance in which it arises. Passion, however, is not a feeling as much as it is a perspective, an enthusiasm for all things that nourish one's soul and inspire the mind to dimensions yet unexplored. The man without such passion quickly falls to apathy and then to some form of suicide.

80

The higher man should possess a bit of a rebellious soul if he is to rise above the status quo. No man ever changed his perception by striding atop a treadmill or circling the grindstone. If he is to truly see the world, he must instead venture to the horizon with a quickened gait, ignoring the pleas of fear that emanate from his more cautious contemporaries. They have traded wisdom for security and they pay the debt of this arrangement by surrendering their souls to a landscape both dull and stagnant — a scenery that suits them well. The higher man, though, must tear himself from this community and journey out alone. For this he will need the kind of spirit more recognized in the eagle than in the sheep.

81

The higher man is interested in the very best of culture because these arts convey the very best of man. High culture is the cultivation of all humanity and, as such, it provides inspiration for a man attempting to cultivate himself — it exhibits a trail which others have taken, reveals an aim perhaps not otherwise devised. The highest elements of culture teach a man how to be civilized, not by some pedantic means, but by revealing the essence of man at his most splendid — at his highest powers of reason and imagination combined. The finest music, philosophy, painting, poetry and prose on display in all its grandeur for man's enjoyment and edification. The lower elements of culture exist primarily to titillate and amuse, appealing to the baser qualities of a man, his more animal nature. Thus, they chiefly attract the lower man, but teach him little about his higher self — content instead to stir his less subtle emotions. In this manner, a man is inspired to intensity instead of passion and he begins to make a spectacle of his sentimentality — essentially returning him to childhood.

82

Boredom in the life of a man, although inevitable to a certain degree, will really only persist for he who is not living as he would wish.

83

They are dismissed as misanthropes who would hold man accountable for the consequences of his delusions, the outcomes of his stupidity and ignorance, and the ramifications of his indifference. They are expected instead, with a tender heart and something of a sentimental fidelity, to direct their view to man's more positive qualities, as if holding him to a higher standard is far too much to ask. Yet, in perceiving mankind's more virtuous traits, one becomes keenly aware of mankind's possibilities and immediately is struck by how many men fail in even *attempting* to achieve such promise.

84

Wisdom is often recognized only in relation to the man who is lacking in it.

85

True freedom, the attainment of character, and the achievement of the higher man's perspective are accessible to most men yet realized by only the very few chiefly because mankind is so easily distracted and so readily prone to surrender when faced with the challenge of uncertainty.

86

The higher man may pledge temporary allegiance to any number of agencies or institutions as long as these associations benefit the essential project that he wishes to undertake. He should feel free, however, to abandon these allegiances at the moment they no longer serve his purpose since the overall concern is for his vital endeavors. The lesser man, of course, must pledge everlasting allegiance to the institution because he has no overreaching and fundamental ventures for his existence and serves not his inner nature but an external corporation which provides him with rules, dogma, and prepackaged understanding with which to order an otherwise disorderly and meaningless existence.

87

It's not that one can necessarily blame a man for wanting to avoid the seemingly bleak and despairing truth of the cosmos by hiding himself in comforting illusions, distractions, or rational justifications. The higher man, though, recognizes these as somewhat cowardly, or at the very least, immature, responses to adversity. Additionally, these methods prevent a more sublime and profound understanding of the universe. The lower man, perhaps, was born to these aversions — it may simply not suit his character to view the world as might an artist. The higher man, though he may share none of the artist's skill, may still participate in the artist's perception.

88

The higher man has no desire for tyranny or political power of any kind. He surely recognizes that men are sometimes driven by their darker natures and so must be controlled by law, especially the politician.

89

The great man must strive to free himself from all allegiances that fail to improve him; all ideologies that require that he should mindlessly serve; all relations with other men that disappoint the profundity of his spirit; and all activities that lull him into a waking slumber or merely serve to stroke the great egotistical beast.

90

Hedonism seems a perfectly logical response to a world devoid of universal absolutes and driving purpose. Yet, such a man, who would succumb to the comforts of pleasure and the satisfactions of desire (superficial though they be) as a kind of doctrine by which he governs his life, must also accept his status as something no more unique than any other animal that forages on the earth. Only the higher man is uniquely human, though his status as such should also provide no further privilege than its own reward.

91

The great man will never "find his place" in society or "fit in" to any significant degree. He may, if the fates allow, find himself among a small band of like minded souls, but for the most part he will travel the world alone. Such a thought strikes terror into the heart of the common man, but to the uncommon spirit it is something of a preference.

92

The great man, if he is to remain sound in heart and mind, must eventually come to terms with the fact that he will be only marginally, at best, accepted by his contemporaries. His faith must reside in himself and his projects. This is his true salvation in life. Chasing the approval and love of his contemporaries will only serve to lower himself in his own estimation. Yet, whether he is lionized, vilified, or forgotten by future generations is, likewise, an immaterial thing since all shall eventually fade from the memory of the world. He is left with the integrity of the moment alone.

93

The majority of human beings act in their lives for the sake of their own happiness, or what they believe to be their happiness anyway. The great man, on the other hand, acts for the sake of his own individual excellence as a human being — though it may bring him at times sorrow, misery, dissatisfaction, and the inability to successfully flourish in his time. What he will find instead is integrity, wisdom, and the deepest connection with that which is truly eternal.

94

The only thing that the great man knows with certainty is that all which he now holds to be true may, in some future time, prove to be something which is either only partially true or entirely false. This does not fill him with dread because it affords the possibility of greater awareness, which is his primary goal, and it does not fill him with resignation because, although he does not harbor the naïve hope that he will ever come to an understanding of ultimate truth, he does possess the belief that tomorrow shall find him wiser than he is today.

95

Only the content of one's character should determine the higher man. Yet, as soon as such a man begins to wield this superiority as some kind of instrument of power, he proves himself unworthy of it.

96

The destiny of the higher man is not found trudging along the paths of wealth, honor, and fame. He follows, instead, the trail of greater awareness so that each step along the way increases his vitality and enables him to grow intellectually, spiritually, morally, and artistically in one way or another, for he knows that life is an aesthetic and intellectual experience whose goal has as its end the acquisition of wisdom rather than materials.

97

The higher man is neither a builder of nations nor a leader of them, though he is responsible for shaping higher culture to a certain degree. He is, primarily, a beacon for those brave individuals who, like himself, have set out to sea alone, away from the mainland of base humanity, in search of a greater understanding of himself and the world.

98

True friendship can only develop, indeed *should* only develop, between two equals in character and intelligence. The great man, then, should prepare himself to spend a great deal of time alone with his books.

99

It's imperative for the wise man to find a means of passing along his wisdom — lest he prove himself unwise by hoarding it all for himself.

100

The lives of higher men are more often spent in the dim light of relative obscurity, which suits them to a certain degree, living as they do in the realm of the mind. If they must suffer the inhumanity of fame, it usually occurs posthumously, if at all. More often than not, their funerals are ill attended though their graves may be well received. Their contemporaries are usually unaware of the orchid that grew amidst the weeds.

101

The great man creates his own religion, purged of all disciples and governed merely upon the principles of his own better nature.

102

The great man must first be called to his task, then he must hear it, accept it, and begin to work fervently to accomplish it. Contrary to popular opinion, *all* men are called to the service of the divine, but few are aware enough in their everyday lives to perceive the summons and fewer still accept it — the rest retreat to religion. Those who then do make the commitment to pursue this path must remain light-heartedly steadfast and conscientious to the cause; otherwise he will eventually surrender his resolve —it not being something that is quickly or easily achieved. It is this kind of stamina that is essential for the man of character. The rest of mankind will find their home among the religious, the superstitious, the hedonists, and the charlatans.

103

Contrary to Nietzsche's belief, the higher man is not harmed by the traditional conceptions of morality. He is continually surrounded by laws, rules, and beliefs that he finds to be distasteful, ignorant, and even perhaps unjust altogether — directives that, if accepted, would certainly lead to a weakening of his spirit — opposed as they are to the dynamic nature of the soul itself. A truly great man, however, will be acutely aware that it is the continual confrontation with these stultifying forces which helps to shape his character. He instinctively knows that he must rebel.

104

The great man must learn to endure if he is to remain unspoiled by the common world of men. His victories will seem small by comparison since the work of charlatans is that which is most celebrated, but he must maintain a faith in himself and a commitment to his better nature — ignoring the temptations that so easily might stray him from his path.

105

A sense of play is essential for the great man and differs in kind from distraction in that it is a perspective with which to engage the world while distraction merely attempts to escape from it. Nevertheless, playfulness is essential because it is the proper relationship between man and nature.

106

The common man aspires to compete among his contemporaries for power, status, privilege, and money. These are tangible qualities that can be easily accessed by even the most challenged of intellects. In this manner, the common man competes at his own level, against those who can be considered his equals, for the crude and quantifiable prizes of Incorporated modernity. The higher man, similarly, competes with his contemporaries in childhood before learning the value of competing with himself as a young adult. This will eventually lead him, if he is to be a great man, into competition with all of antiquity. The higher man, in other words, evolves.

107

A great man must be first and foremost an iconoclast, but he must always remember that in the wake of his destruction of dogma and tradition will be the displaced refugees of those particular beliefs and customs, who now, though ill equipped to do so, must suddenly learn to swim in frigid waters. He must recognize that not all men, a precious few actually, are committed to truly understanding and of these, even fewer have the strength of character necessary to endure the uncertainties inherent in such a task.

108

Sacrifice is necessary for any great accomplishment, though it does not need to be sacrificing for others, as religion would demand. A sacrifice made to cultivate one's own greatness of character is a worthy ambition as well.

109

The obvious modern illustration of Plato's cave is that of the movie theater where patrons are strapped for all their lives, forced to watch countless images on the screen in front of them while they interpret these facsimiles as reality itself. The philosopher is he who breaks away from these illusions and exits the theater to find the true world. Plato would have him then return to the place from where he came in hopes of rescuing others. Yet, the modern philosopher should not be surprised to discover that, not only will there be those who refuse to leave and others still who will not believe him, once a man emerges from the darkened theater and lets his eyes adjust to the light, he will immediately begin to complain that the colors are too dull and the pace of life too slow. He will yawn continually with boredom, uninspired and wholly unaffected by nature and the world around him, and it will not take long before he will seek to return to his former life of flickering shadows again. The philosopher, then, stands more or less alone among the living. This is all the more reason that he should conduct himself as something of a shining example of character rather than a prophet of truth — in order to inspire those who struggle after him.

110

There's an untamable wildness about the wolf, an inner ferocity of spirit arguably unequaled in all of nature — as well as the magnanimous pride in his bearing, the gracefulness in his step, and the mischievous, lighthearted, even playful manner in which he encounters the world. Yet, he is also an animal of extreme gentleness and affability whose understanding of the necessity for and the acceptance of a natural social order and his role in it shows him much wiser than the majority of men. In these ways and more, the wolf is the ideal symbol of the higher man.

About The Author

Emile Benoit is a writer living in California. He has a B.A. and M.A. in philosophy from San Diego State University.

www.ingramcontent.com/pod-product-compliance
Lightning Source LLC
Chambersburg PA
CBHW031834090426
42741CB00005B/234